D1174670

The Fall of Eben Emael

THE FALL OF EBEN EMAEL

PRELUDE TO DUNKERQUE

By Col. James E. Mrazek (Ret.)

Library of Congress Card Catalog Number 74-110765

CONTENTS

CHRONOLOGY (Belgian time)

10 May 1940

0030 Fort Eben Emael given alert by Headquarters, Liège

0032 Claxons sound alert throughout interior of Fort

0315 Fort's artillery begins firing blank rounds at 30-second intervals to alert countryside to emergency

0330 Eleven gliders transporting Assault Group Granite take off from Ostheim, Germany

0415 Gliders arrive near Fort and cast off from towing airplanes and begin descents towards Fort

0425 Gliders land and glide over assault casemates and cupolas on surface of Fort

0430 Hitler's Blitzkrieg crosses Dutch, Belgian, and French borders

0500 Paratroopers complete missions

0630 Lieutenant Witzig's glider arrives on Fort. Witzig takes over command from Sergeant Wenzel

1000 Belgians begin to counterattack Germans on Fort

1345 Belgian reserves leave Wonck to come to aid of Fort

1530 Belgian reserves from Wonck begin counterattack

2000 Commandant of Fort calls off further counterattacks

2030 Commandant issues operational orders for defense of Fort during the night

11 May 1940

2400-0200	Advance elements of German ground forces reach the glidermen on the Fort
0830	Witzig turns captured installations over to German engineers
0900	Witzig buries dead and leaves Fort
0900	Commandant begins destruction of secret papers
1130	Commandant convenes council to discuss surrender
1145	Belgians open negotiations with Germans

To my children

Jim Jr.

and

Joanne

ACKNOWLEDGMENTS

This book has been made possible through the cooperation of many people. Historian and author Dr. Virgil Ney, and Colonel Brook Nihart, U.S.M.C. (ret.), and now Managing Editor of The Journal of the Armed Forces, were especially helpful in providing me with constructive criticism to improve the manuscript.

I am especially grateful to General a.D. Werner Bodenstein of the Army of the Federal Republic of Germany, and to Mrs. Alice Pennington. General Bodenstein spent many hours translating combat reports, providing me with insights on the operation and technical matters. He also gathered source materials for me in Germany.

Mrs. Pennington gave me the encouragement that helped me to get through those difficult periods many authors find when they write a book. She gave me invaluable assistance in translating many sources published in French and German. She also prepared the glossary and did all the typing.

Miss Dorothy Savage, Miss Evelyn Robinson and Miss Gene Kubal of the Army Library in the Pentagon were most helpful in doing research for me.

I am heavily indebted to Mr. Henri Decluse of Liège, Belgium. He was a private soldier and a member of the crew of casemate nine at Fort Eben Emael when it was attacked. He has a rich collection of memorabilia of Fort Eben Emael and the attack, and has been most generous in making it available to me.

I would be remiss if I did not cite the assistance rendered by Colonel Albert Torreele, Army Attaché of the Belgian Embassy in Washington, D.C. On 10 May 1940 Colonel Torreele, then a lieutenant, was in command of a Belgian platoon sent to drive the German glidermen from the Vroenhoven bridge. He was wounded there. Colonel Torreele has given generous assistance that has helped me to understand the action at the Fort. He reviewed the manuscript and made many constructive suggestions.

I am grateful to Jean-Louis Lhoest, author of "Les Allemandes au Canal Albert" for the use of his excellent book as source material and for his generosity in permitting me to reproduce some of the illustrations therein.

Also, I owe thanks to Mr. Rudolph Opitz, now an engineer with AVCO Corporation in Stratford, Connecticut who provided insights of the history of glider development and the activity in the months prior to 10 May 1940. Mr. Opitz was one of the glider pilots who participated in the operation and flew one of the gliders that landed glidermen to attack one of the bridges.

I appreciate the suggestions offered by Hanna Reitsch.

I owe thanks to the American Army Attaché in Belgium, Colonel Cecil M. Sanders, for enabling me to coordinate my efforts with Belgian military and civilian authorities. I am especially grateful for the assistance provided by the Belgian Army and the permission it gave for me to visit the ruins of Fort Eben Emael.

Finally, I must mention the gracious hospitality shown me by General and Mrs. Kurt Student, Colonel and Mrs. Rudolf Witzig, Oberföerster and Mrs. Helmut Wenzel and also Mr. Jean De Sloovere and his attractive family.

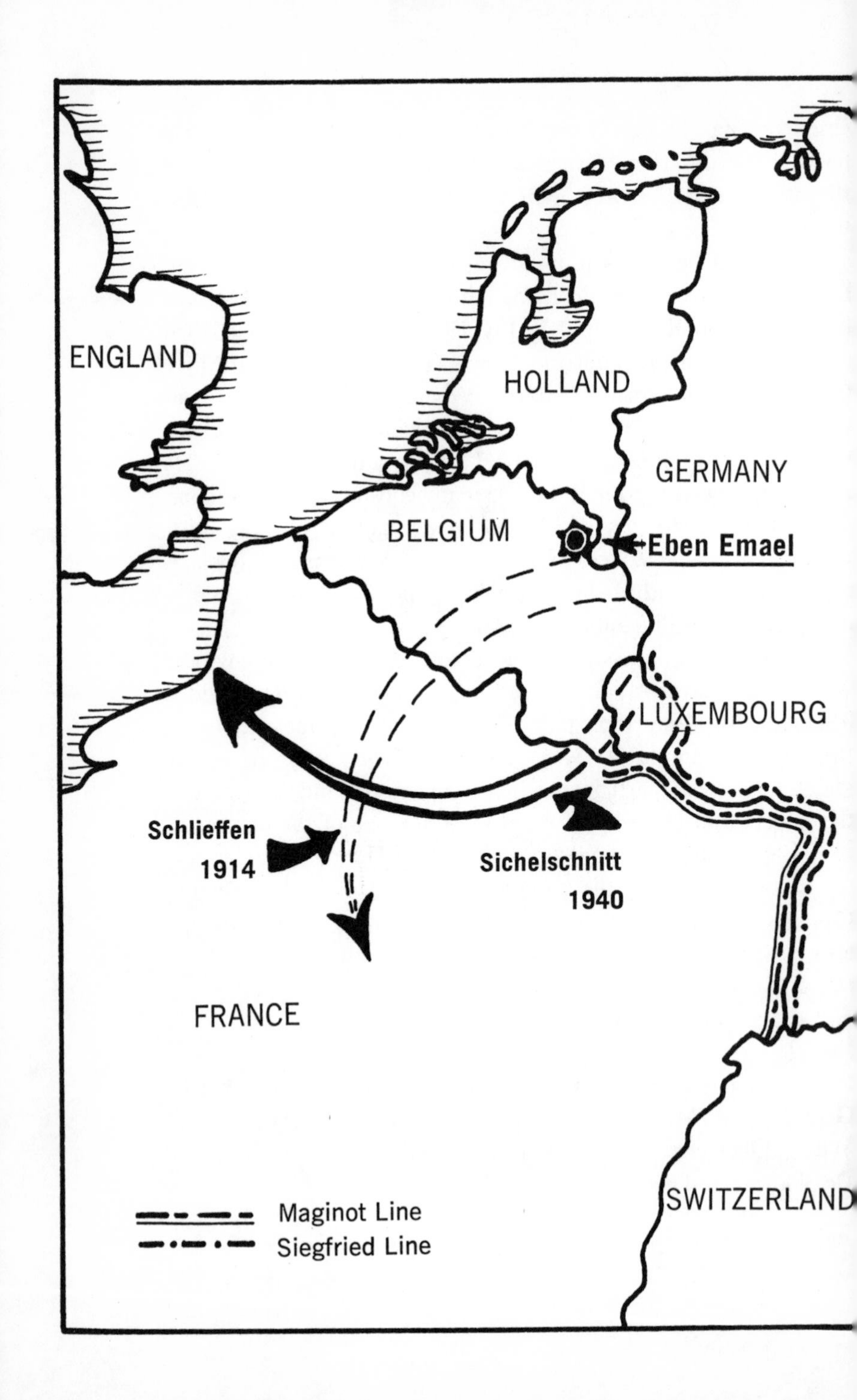
ENGLAND
HOLLAND
GERMANY
BELGIUM
Eben Emael
LUXEMBOURG
Schlieffen
1914
Sichelschnitt
1940
FRANCE
SWITZERLAND
Maginot Line
Siegfried Line

INTRODUCTION

At midday, 11 May 1940, Fort Eben Emael, "impregnable" key to the Belgian defense system, succumbed to an unexpected assault, victim of an untried weapon. In 28 action-packed hours 78 daring German glidermen silenced the Fort. A cowed Belgian garrison *ten times* their number filed from its catacomb-like recesses to become German prisoners for the duration of World War II.

The blow stunned the Belgian nation and startled the world. However, the cataclysmic events that followed soon paled the face of Eben Emael and it gradually faded from memory. For years the military tactics that defeated this fortress have remained obscure, even to most Germans.

Once Fort Eben Emael had been conquered, German panzers surged through the gap created in the Belgian defenses. The Belgian situation deteriorated rapidly. The fortress city of Liège surrendered one day later. The impact of the fast-paced uncontrollable events, so demoralized the Belgians that King Leopold III capitulated on 27 May 1940, precipitating the British debacle at Dunkerque. Approaches to the rear of the Maginot line now lay unprotected against Wehrmacht envelopment. On 22 June a doomed France surrendered, unable to stem the onrushing blitzkrieg swinging in behind the vaunted Maginot fortifications.

The multimillion dollar Fort Eben Emael should have held indefinitely against any conventional assault. Had it repelled attack for even a few months, or at least six days, as the French had hoped, the whole course of the war might have been altered. Certainly, French mobile forces, poised at the northern extremity of the Maginot line and bolstered by Belgium's reserves, would have counterattacked towards Fort Eben Emael. Backed by British Expeditionary Forces, the whole Allied line might have recoiled and turned back the onslaught. The sudden collapse of the Allied military power and the political alliance behind it would have been forestalled, if not prevented.

Had the Germans fought conventionally, as their adversaries expected, they might have won a conventional victory, at the cost of heavy bloodshed, after many months of grueling combat. If Fort Eben Emael had held as it should have, German armies would have had to operate through the Ardennes, south of the Fort, then arc north to the coast to consummate the "Sichelschnitt" (cut of the sickle) strategy.

But the Germans did not fight according to the books, at least not on that initial day of the invasion of the West. With several secret weapons, they introduced a new style of dynamic warfare.

Accounts of the Fort's capture published in English to date are scant, and unfortunately, rife with inaccuracies. Some of these accounts are derived from early German reports which, because of official silence on the operation, contain more conjecture than fact. For example, the authorized garrison for the fort was 1,200 men and this is the figure used by most historians. In fact, the Germans caught the garrison undermanned by more than 400.

What really happened? Was there collusion with the enemy in high military circles, was there incompetence in the Belgian High Command, or were the Belgian defenses ruptured because of unforeseeable changes in the miltary art?

1. BELGIUM'S GEOGRAPHIC DILEMMA

Belgium has always been less a military prize than a geographical unfortunate. It temptingly offers some of the best terrain and facilities in northern Europe for tank and motorized columns. Gently undulating vistas of neatly cultivated fields and lush emerald pastures checkerboard the countryside. Belgium is intersected by the best roads and railroads connecting the political centers of two historical military rivals, Germany and France.

Although Belgian fear of being trampled under has been periodically assuaged by international agreements that were to give it, as a buffer state between great military powers, a neutral status in case of war, it has never felt secure. Cities west of the German-Belgian border, such as Liège, Brussels and Paris, provided tempting military and political objectives for German expansion and made the Belgian position unavoidably precarious. Beginning in the late 19th century, the German General Staff accorded the "Belgian Problem" priority attention in any plans calling for the invasion of France. Belgium could be either a sluice gate to pour German forces into France, or a dike to hold back a military advance. But it could not be both.

By the turn of the century, a realistic German General Staff concluded that Germany might have to fight a French-Russian military coalition. Vastly outnumbered German armies would have to tackle the awesomely large Czarist armies in the east and the French Army in the west which was spoiling for a chance to wipe out its embarrassing defeat in the Franco-Prussian War (1870-71). Although Germany had the military advantage of interior lines that would enable her to shift forces to counter either army, 1,000 miles separated the two which presented difficult logistic problems. As a solution, Count Alfred von Schlieffen, Chief of the German General Staff from 1891 to 1905, developed a daring and original plan of operation, thereafter to bear his name. Analyzing Hannibal's great victory at Cannae he fashioned a bold offensive plan combining an encirclement and double envelopment of the French Army.

Von Schlieffen concluded that any frontal attack of French positions would be bloody and time consuming and of questionable military strategy. Britain could be expected to rush armies to bolster French lines. Vast Czarist armies, given time to mobilize, could attack and imperil Germany on the east. Searching for a strategy less costly than the frontal attack, von Schlieffen considered a maneuver around the flanks of the French positions. One route led through the Swiss Alps, a formidable geographic obstacle to a modern army. The other route crossed Belgium, providing excellent facilities for a mass army to move quickly.

Von Schlieffen seized upon a bold strategy. A modest 10-division German army was to parry the Czarist hordes. With an agglomeration of Germany's prime military power, he planned a swift thrust through Belgium to the French army's northern flank to paralyze France before British armies could cross the English Channel to bolster French lines. Thus, years before 1914, Belgium's doom was sealed in the war rooms of the German Staff.

Between 1893 and 1905, although changed in detail, the plan maintained the thrust of an overwhelming strong German right wing through Belgium to get behind the French, disorganize them, and thus enable another German force from the south to join in staging a vast Hannibalian drama.

Although publicly bound to a national policy of neutrality and a faint hope that Germany would respect it, the Belgians also had to be realistic. German expansionists had to be reckoned with. General Henri Brailmont, army engineer and Belgium's "Vauban," constructed a stout defense system before World War I. Immense forts ringed with outer defensive works arose at Liège, Namur and Antwerp. These would hold against German guns until Belgium could mobilize and, with the aid of France, make a coordinated counter attack.

On 3 August 1914, Germany declared war on France and arbitrarily demanded that tiny Belgium allow German armies unhindered passage. Belgium refused. The Kaiser's Imperial Chancellor, Dr. von Bethmann-Hollweg, brushed aside the Neutrality Treaty of 1839 as a "scrap of paper". The Germans crossed the border and struck so violently that Liège, the key fort, and its ring of 12 outer forts fell in 11 days. Other forts yielded. The way to France lay open. Four bitter years of war followed.

As the nineteen-twenties turned into the thirties a succession of ominous events occurred. On 14 October 1933 Germany deserted the League of Nations. In 1934 Nazi conspirators assassinated Englebert Dollfuss, Chancellor of Austria. By the end of that year the National Socialist party had come to power in Germany and Adolf Hitler had become Fuehrer. A recrudescent Germany, seething under defeat, again began to cause alarm in plucky little Belgium. The Belgians began to wonder how long Germany would abide by the arms limitations placed on her by the 1918 Armistice.

On 10 May, 1935, Hitler rejected the Armistice and Germany reinstituted conscription and began to rearm. The swelling tide of Hitlerism became an increasing threat to the peace that had cost Belgium so heavily in World War I.

But the Belgians were not sitting idly by. Albert I, King of Belgium, had vowed with the firm support of Parliament to stand firm along its borders against any attack. An indomitable defense against another German invasion could be guaranteed by the construction of a massive fort in a hill mass at the junction of the Albert Canal and the Meuse River.

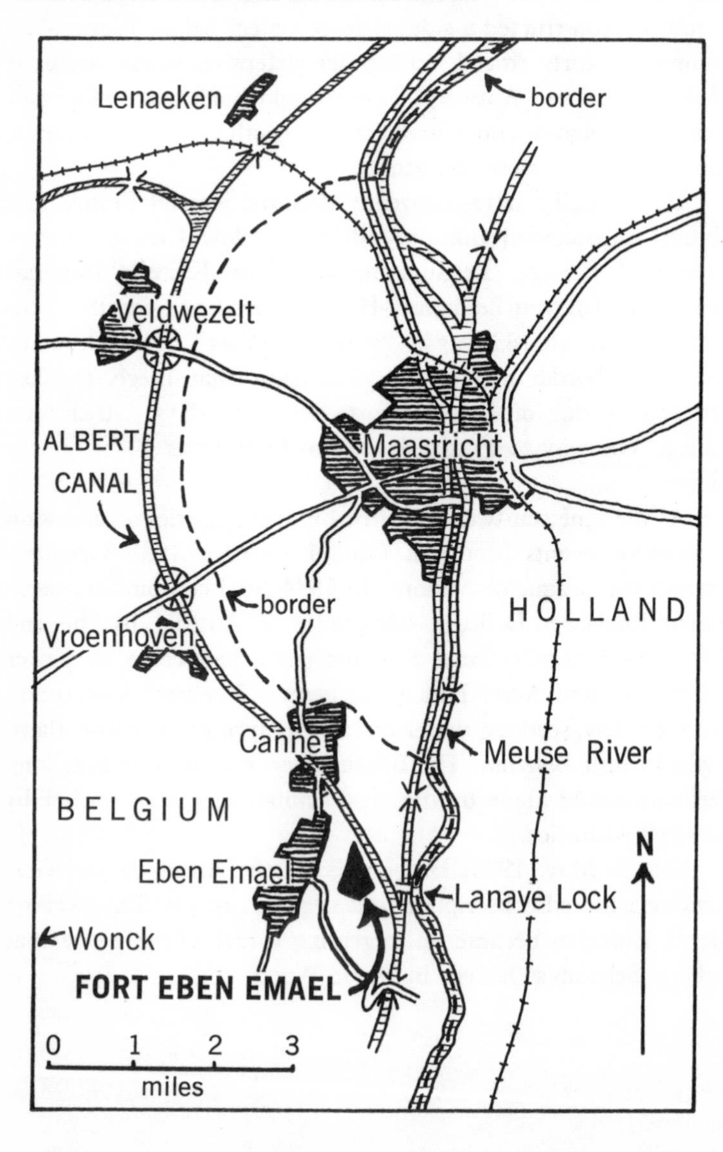

2. THE IMPREGNABLE FORTRESS

The decision to stand resolutely at the juncture of the Meuse River and the Albert Canal had some merit in a tactical sense. As early as 1887 General Brailmont had sought the construction of a strong fort in the general vicinity, but the Belgian government turned a deaf ear.

On 4 August 1914, General von Kluck's 1st Army, of 260,000 strong, crossed the Meuse at Lixhe just two miles south of the recommended site. The Kaiser's World War I invasion plan depended upon their unimpeded march through Belgium. They met slight local resistance at Lixhe and the artillery fire from Belgian Forts Barchon and Pontisse, four miles south, proved inaccurate and did not slow the German crossing. If a fort had been built at Eben Emael prior to World War I, it might have slowed the crossing at Lixhe, made von Kluck more cautious, and perhaps even deflected his main effort.

In 1927 the Belgium government decided to build a canal which would compete with the newly constructed Dutch Juliana Canal used to transport large cargoes to and from northern ports. The Belgians, in surveying routes for their canal, decided to connect it to the Meuse at the Lanaye lock three miles south of Maastricht. At Lanaye, however, the Belgians faced an imposing task. The hill mass along the Belgian side overlooking Lanaye, known as Caster, rose a precipitous 200 feet. Nevertheless they chose this route and in less than two years engineers had knifed through the limestone mass down to the Lanaye level. The excavations were equal in magnitude to cuts at Suez, Egypt and at Culebra in the Isthmus of Panama.

When completed, the Belgians had their canal plus a first-rate dividend, a superb site for a fort, some of its defenses ready made. The near perpendicular wall of the Albert Canal on the northeast, and the cliff along the Meuse to the south provided excellent protection for two flanks. The site was a Vauban-minded designer's dream giving an unparalleled view of miles of countryside towards Germany.

Thus, in 1928 when General A. G. Galet proposed a fort at this point to a Royal Commission studying the Belgian defense systems, the merits of the idea were already so apparent, reinforced by the sobering results of General von Kluck's invasion in World War I, that the idea won the Commission's support at once. Thus Brailmont was vindicated.

Three years later Parliament appropriated 35,000,000 Belgian francs to close the defense gap around Lixhe by building a fort described by M. Albert Diveze, the Minister of National Defense, as ". . . able to withstand the pounding of the heaviest artillery." In 1931, the year construction started on the Albert Canal, surveyors with transit on shoulder, core drillers noisily pulsating in the distance, and an assortment of military brass began the gradual disruption of the tranquility of village and countryside.

Close on the heels of these interlopers, came construction contractors with their heavy cement mixers and many kinds of construction machinery. Muffled explosions deep underground rattled crockery, drove frightened ravens flapping into the sky and shook chunks of aged and brittle russet tile from rooftops. United Enterprises, a huge Belgian combine, one of many firms to bid, received the contract to erect the Fort. Ironically, not having all the technical skills and other resources needed for such a prodigious task, its directors called two German companies, A. G. Hochtief of Essen, and Dycherhoff and Widmann of Wiesbaden into the project as subcontractors.

Colonel Jean Mercier, of the Belgian Army Corps of Engineers, had charge of the construction. The first shovel of earth was turned in April 1932. From then on Mercier kept construction moving at a relentless pace until the task was completed in 1935.

The Fort was named Eben Emael after a nearby village. Nothing about the town of Eben Emael suggests that it would be etched into the pages of history. Hidden away in a vale more than a mile from the fort that took its name, was a forgotten village in its early days, the origin of its name not known although some say it is inherited from several prehistoric caves close by, now turned to growing mushrooms. There are no Roman walls, no siege defenses, nothing to suggest a military lineage. Like many sites now famous in history, particularly military history, Eben Emael stumbled upon fame.

Fort Eben Emael bore no resemblance to peaceful Eben Emael, the village. The village, in fact, was really two villages, Eben and Emael, that time and growth merged. There is little logic in having named the Fort "Eben Emael" as the heart of the village is almost a mile away. (We are reminded of the battle site "Waterloo". Napoleon Bonaparte was actually defeated in 1815 at La Haye Sainte. Waterloo, two miles north, was the postmark on a dispatch the Duke of Wellington sent to London telling of his victory).

The melancholy fort, its somber grey battlements deeply scarred, resembled a menacing arrowhead pointed at Maastricht. It sat above the angle created by the steep side of the Albert Canal, which forms the high west wall of the Fort, and the narrow serpentine Geer (Jaar) River, 150 yards to the east. Sharply inclined, reinforced concrete embankments join the Fort to the wall of the Albert Canal. The Belgians used every military artifice to add strength to the natural defenses of the Canal, the Geer River and the elevated terrain. Row on row of barbed wire, interspersed with triangular steel antitank obstacles, and mine fields, encircled the walls. Infantry, at outlying positions were to cover these defenses by rifle and machine gun fire and were also to serve as the first line of defense of the Fort against an enemy attack. Defenders could place massed artillery fires on threatening enemy formations when the need occurred.

A 450-yard concrete-lined, water-filled moat, starting at the Albert Canal, accentuated the defense of the west wall. Huge steel-reinforced concrete casemates, like medieval caponieres jutted from the walls at critical points. When the Fort was in its prime, sixty-millimeter antitank guns and machine guns, poked through the embrasures to shoot flanking fire along the walls to destroy any enemy attempting to scale the walls after penetrating the cordons of Belgian infantry, the rows of barbed wire and the mine fields.

The platform within the walls measured 1,100 yards from north to south and 800 yards at its widest point, space enough to play 70 American football games simultaneously. The Fort had three levels of installations, each level with its own unique function. Dome-shaped, heavily armored steel cupolas, massive concrete casemates and antiaircraft guns protruded above the surface of the ground comprising the topmost level. To create deceptive strength, engineers inserted two dummy cupolas at the north end of the Fort and one at the south end. A command post, a hospital, isolated ammunition storage caves, six 175-hp electrical generators to power guns, elevators and lights, and a signal center occupied mid level. The bottom level had chambers used as barracks. Wide stairs, elevators for ammunition bearers and

A dummy cupola at Eben Emael before the attack.

ammunition hoists directly to guns enabled rapid servicing of the weapons in cupolas and casemates. Air conditioning units assured a liveable environment, pumping heated air through the vast underground complex at all times for, even in summer, without heat it became cellar cold and dank in the tunnels. Cupolas and casemates were similar in size, machinery and organization to the mechanism necessary to service and operate a multiple-gun turret of a modern cruiser or battleship. The crew for these emplacements consisted of 16 men for the smaller ones to 30 men for the largest, casemate position nine.

The entrance to a casemate or cupola was at the same level as the tunnel floor leading to the work. Usually, the ammunition chamber was at this level across the tunnel from the entryway. Just inside the entryway, between the entrance from the tunnel and the base of the emplacement itself were two thick, heavily-riveted steel doors six feet apart. The doors closed towards each other. Between the doors and along each side, were two 8-inch slots, two feet apart from floor to ceiling. Standing close by were eight-inch steel I beams. These beams could be lowered into slots on the wall opposite the doors to form a steel barrier.

If an enemy penetration was expected the doors nearest the casemate well could be closed and locked, then a wall of steel beams inserted, then a layer of sandbags placed in the two-foot interval and then the second steel door closed and locked from the tunnel side. This ingenious arrangement could rapidly deny access to the interior of the Fort, should an enemy succeed in penetrating even one emplacement.

The Fort had two artillery batteries. One was for offensive fire, the other defensive. Over the years, the Belgians worked out a comprehensive system of artillery fire, anticipating every enemy threat. Because the concept of Belgian neutrality had to be respected by the Belgian High Command, targets of enemy infantry, tanks, or other forces for the artillery had to be within

Belgian territory before they could be fired upon. Thus, the guns of casemates twelve and eighteeen were to cover areas in Belgium along the Belgian-Dutch border south of Maastricht, particularly the bridges at Vroenhoven, Veltwezelt and Canne. These bridges were extremely sensitive, providing enemy access to the heart of the country. The artillery had to support the Belgian infantry which protected these bridges by preventing the enemy from getting close to or taking them. If the bridges fell to the enemy, the Fort's artillery had to fire on and destroy the bridges. The fact that the enemy might try to cross the Meuse over pontoon bridges was also foreseen and Belgian fire plans were made to cover all approaches where such an attempt might be made. Similar plans existed for the area south of the Fort lying in Belgian territory. Thus, the 75-mm guns of casemates twenty-six and nine fired to the south and had the primary mission of placing fire around the critical Belgian city of Visé.

Twenty-three, thirty-one and twenty-four were revolvable twin gun cupolas with steel domes 12 inches thick. To fire, the guns and the domes of the first two could be raised up four feet above the level of the top of the casemate into which they were set. The combination was retracted into the casemate to relay and load the guns. Twenty-four housed two 120-mm guns, the Fort's heaviest punch. The guns protruded through two apertures in the dome which did not elevate as the others. These steel-shielded guns added the ultimate in versatility and power to the artillery and could take an enemy under fire anywhere within a 12 mile radius.

The second battery was defensive and largely existed for the protection of the heavy, offensive guns. The guns of this battery were mounted in the caponiere-like casemates set around the perimeter of the Fort. Three other installations on the surface had weapons to fire at an enemy endangering the surface. One of these consisted of four pairs of multiple-mount antiaircraft machine guns, each set in a dugout. The second and third were machine guns in casemates set into embankments on the northern part of the Fort. Observation post Eben I was the main observation dome and was an integral part of artillery cupola thirty-one. It had unobstructed vision in all directions except to a limited extent towards the north where a small woods on the Fort cut off vision.

The Fort had an authorized strength of 1,200 officers and men. The Regiment of the Fortress of Liège was the next higher command. In brief ceremonies held in the autumn of 1934 and carried on amid construction turmoil, Major Decoux, Captain A. Hotermans and a cadre of officers and enlisted men took charge of the Fort's operable facilities.

On 10 May 1940 the official strength of the first battery stood at 206 officers and men. However, because some men were on leave, others ill in the hospital or officially absent taking artillery courses, the battery was 25 per cent under strength. Of 242 for the second battery, 79 were absent, making this unit 32 per cent under strength. Thus, the Fort had 18 officers, 62 non-commissioned officers and 570 enlisted ranks to make a total of 650. There were 233 in a relief force at Wonck. Although authorized to be commanded by a lieutenant colonel, Major Jean Fritz Lucien Jottrand, a regular officer of many years service was in command on May 10, 1940.

Coupled with the protection to this area of the border provided by the Fort's weapons systems, every bridge over the Canal and locks along it were prepared for destruction. The Belgians mined the concrete footings and girders. Overlooking each bridge stood a menacing casemate whose crew kept a round-the-clock vigil of the bridge. From the Casemates wires ran to the charges set into the bridges and the crews, at the proper signal or order, or on their own initiative if the need arose, were to destroy the bridges.

Major Jottrand was charged with the responsibility for destroying the bridges at Canne and Petit Lanaye and the Canal locks at Lanaye. Another Belgian officer, located in a headquarters in a military caserne at Lanaeken, was charged with destroying the bridges at Vroenhoven and Veltwezelt.

Colonel Albert Torreele, Belgian Attaché to the United States, reminiscing with the author, gave his impression of the Fort in 1938 when, as a young lieutenant, he toured it with his class from the École Royale Militaire, the Belgian Army's equivalent of our West Point.

> An officer member of the garrison of the Fort led us to many of the outer defenses and showed what each was intended for. We went to the walls and looked over countless rows of barbed wire. He led us to the only door on the surface set deep in concrete. It appeared like the heavy steel door of a bank vault. From here infantry in reserve would issue to repel any enemy fortunate enough to get by the tough ground defenses.
>
> He took us deep into the interior and we trudged many miles to the end of the tunnels, visiting the crews and the guns of emplacements we had seen at the surface. Crews gave us their missions and detailed characteristics of their guns. All was very professional. Later, we assembled in the Command Post. The Commandant gave a detailed account of how he proposed to defend the Fort in event of an attack. I got the impression of tremendous power and first-rate efficiency. *I was convinced nothing could happen!* (Author's italics).

View of the village of Eben Emael from casemate 23.

General Kurt Student—circa 1940.

3. A MATTER OF UTMOST URGENCY!

General Kurt Student, intently making a point to the unit commanders in his newly activated 7th Flieger (airborne) Division, glanced quizzically at his aide who had just come to his side. It was mid afternoon, 27 October 1939.

The aide had disobeyed orders. General Student had been specific. Under no circumstances should he be disturbed in this important meeting!

The intense, bespectacled general, no Prussian martinet or Nazi die-hard, but a strong German nationalist, stood unique in the Nazi military hierarchy. General Student was in and out of favor with Hitler many times, but nevertheless, the Fuehrer always seemed to come back to Student who, like General Heinz Guderian and Erwin Rommel, was daring and innovative. Student had had a long and honorable military career. He began his service flying observation aircraft on the Eastern Front in World War I. He flew many missions in support of Field Marshal Paul von Hindenburg's attack against vast Russian forces at Tannenberg. Later, transferred to the Western Front, he flew a bomber at Verdun. In the latter part of the war, as a fighter pilot, he downed five French aircraft in the Champagne sector of France. He was a captain when the war ended, and transferred to the infantry after the war. In 1934, after an assignment in the Air Defense Branch of the Reichswehr, he returned to the Luftwaffe and served in several important posts. He knew the Russians well and did not underrate them as a military force as did many of his contemporaries. He visited the Lipstsk airfield in the U.S.S.R. every year from 1924 to 1928 to observe Soviet air maneuvers. In 1921 he flew his first sport glider and became an avid enthusiast of this sport.

Because of General Student's long association with the Air Forces, his varied career and experiments with parachuting and the transportation of units and supplies by aircraft, Hitler gave him command of the 7th Flieger Division, the world's first airborne division. It was in this capacity in the fall of 1939, when an aide gingerly placed a boldly-written note on the desk in front of him. It read: "Marschal Goering, (Chief of the German Luftwaffe) is on the telephone about a matter of the utmost urgency:"

Student raised the telephone. "This is General Student, Herr Marschall."

"Student," Goering responded, "General Halder (General Franz Halder, Hitler's Army Chief of Staff) just left my office. Der Fuehrer wishes you to visit him alone and without delay."

General Student waved his commanders from the office.

"Herr Marschall, can you tell me the purpose?"

The chubby Goering, no martinet either and a personal fighter pilot friend from World War I days, answered, "Student, I can give you absolutely no clues. I have absolutely nothing. The whole matter is a damned mystery to Halder, too. When can you start?"

"Twenty minutes. I should be in Berlin by 1400."

"Good. Report to me. I am standing by."

General Student buttoned his tunic, grabbed his cap and passed by his officers standing stiffly at attention in the outer office. Turning to his Chief of Staff, "Order my Storch warmed ıp at once. Dismiss the officers ten minutes after I leave this ffice," and, bending closer, "I am on my way to Berlin. No one lse is to be told my destination."

General Student at the controls, his copilot aide at his side, lew into Templehof at exactly 1318. A nondescript looking mousine stood waiting and whisked him to the Reich Chan-ellery and Goering who wasted little time on amenities.

"The Fuehrer is waiting."

Clicking heels resounded in the corridors as sentries suc-essively snapped to attention. Bypassing General Halder, Goer-ıg took General Student directly to Hitler's chambers where the 'uehrer's secretary motioned Goering to an overstuffed chair. 'he secretary then led the thoroughly puzzled General Student ı to the Fuehrer. At the far end of the long walnut paneled oom Hitler raised his eyes from his desk. He returned the "Heil Iitler" and beckoned General Student to look at the map on ıis desk. He allowed the general to study it for several minutes.

"For the war in the West, . . ." Hitler paused, seeming to onsider how to begin, "I know you have made some tests with liders. You have gliders in your division."

General Student nodded and Hitler continued, "I have a ob for you. I want to know if you can do it." He paused again. 'The Belgians have a fort here," and Hitler pointed to its loca-ion on the map. "Do you know it?"

"Yes, Mein Fuehrer, I know it well. It is a tremendous ortification."

Hitler continued:

"The top is like a large grassy field. It has some surface ortifications—I have reports there are heavy artillery gun cupolas ınd casemates—some machine guns. But I have no extensive letails." (Hitler was frequently known to have an excellent grasp of military details and on many occasions seemed better informed on operations than some of his generals.) "I have read something of your work with gliders, General Student. You have been a glider pilot since the early '20's, I believe. I know you have personally flown the attack glider in tests."

"I have an idea. I think some of your attack gliders could land on top of Fort Eben Emael and your men could storm these works. Is that possible?" Hitler looked at him.

To Student, the daring idea sounded both incredible and simple. He said, "I'm not sure. I must think about it. Give me some time."

Hitler nodded, but pressed Student for an early answer, without explaining that he wanted to attack France in late midsummer, 1939, and that he had to have confirmation of Student's ability to participate.

Student returned the next day. Hitler seemed tense and unreceptive to aimless discussion. Without delay Student came to the point. Hitler could see the answer in the glow of General Student's eyes.

"Yes, Mein Fuehrer. It is possible under special circumstances."

Hitler looked at Student, and asked in a warm, moderate tone: "What are the circumstances?"

"The landings must be made in daylight—at least in the morning twilight—not before," replied the general.

"Good! It will be done your way," Hitler affirmed.

"Then, may I have your order?" General Student asked.

Student was in for another surprise. Hitler seemed not to hear the request but sat down and waved Student to a chair. Hitler then told him that during World War I as a soldier he had remembered hearing how the Germans had taken the Belgian Fort Douaumont. The Fort had stood valiantly against repeated German attacks. It was not until the Germans moved siege guns within range and began pounding the Fort to bits that the garrison surrendered. He had studied the operation many times over the years since then. It was not really German heroism that had won, it was the large explosives delivered by the heavy guns that broke Belgian resistance.

Student was well aware of this episode, and concluded that the Fuehrer was merely passing the time of the day to gain a greater rapport with the man to whom he was to entrust such an important task, when suddenly Hitler came to the point. Student got his second and greatest surprise. Hitler had not been wasting time. His discussion of Douaumont had a very serious purpose. He now revealed to the general that German munitions experts had developed a fantastic explosive, a "Hohlladung" (hollow charge). Hitler briefly described it. It was an explosive that could blow through any known military armament, be it steel or concrete. The problem was that it weighed 110 pounds. It could not be shot from a cannon. It had to be put in place, fused, and exploded by two or three men. If it could be delivered to the enemy positions then *nothing, nothing* could withstand it.

If Hitler was correct in his description of the charge's force, the success of the operation was guaranteed. General Student had been concerned about how a few glider loads of men with conventional explosives could really capture Fort Eben Emael. The operation now took on new dimensions and possibilities. Hitler told General Student that he had been trying to solve the problem of how to get the hollow charges to the Fort. Gliders were the solution and, moreover, gliders were silent. Hitler was convinced that this combination of the glider and the hollow charge was unbeatable. When this discussion came to an end Student said again, "Mein Fuehrer, may I now have your order?"

Hitler replied, *"Yes. I order you to take Fort Eben Emael!"* And Hitler told General Student he could consider this verbal order as final. "Remember," Hitler added slowly and deliberately, *"All aspects of the operation must be kept absolutely secret!"*

Hitler knew secrets had a way of getting out. This one would not. He had experienced the doubts of generals who were eager to discredit his daring plans as "hair-brained." Many were all too ready to scoff at the "Little Corporal", a nickname given him because of his rank in World War I.

General Student left. As he later remarked, "I now had a very great responsibility. I could be called to account if the attack failed."

On the glider landings hinged the timing of Germany's ground onslaught. So as not to give away the surprise of the glider landing, the invasion was set for 0430 Belgian time, five minutes after the landings. Thus a glider attack that was to involve a mere 85 men determined the timing for a major invasion. Hitler kept his pledge to land the gliders in daylight despite vehement protests from some of his top generals who fretted at being hampered from starting the invasion before dawn because of what seemed a mere whim of their Fuehrer .

In addition to the Fort Eben Emael operation Hitler gave Student three other tasks. He was to capture the Albert Canal bridges at Canne, Vroenhoven and Veltwezelt with glider assaults, before the Belgians could blow them up to stop the advance of German ground units at the Canal.

The next day an SS officer courier arrived at Student's headquarters carrying a polished black leather pouch. He insisted that he must turn it over to General Student and no one else. It contained the attack order.

The strike at Fort Eben Emael took the code name "Granite." It is not widely known that Hitler alone conceived the attack. It demonstrated Hitler's intuitive and prescient mind, and proved that his ideas could be successful when implemented by dedicated, loyal, willing-to-understand subordinates. It is fortunate for the Allies there were not too many like General Student at Hitler's side.

4. FORGING THE SPEARHEAD

Glider Development

In 1922 Hermann Goering confided to American Captain "Eddie" Rickenbacker, American World War I Ace:

> Our Germany's whole future is in the air, and it is by air power that we are going to recapture the German Empire. To accomplish this we will do three things. First, we will teach gliding *as a sport* to all our young men. Then we will build up commercial aviation. Finally, we will create the skeleton of a military air force. When the time comes, we will put all three together—and the German Empire will be reborn.

As a result the glider played a vital role in Germany's rearmament. It enabled the Germans to train thousands of glider pilots. From this pool the Luftwaffe drew many of its future pilots.

From 1930 to 1933 new trends took place in the development and use of the glider in Germany. A decision was made to design and build a somewhat enlarged sport glider that could be used to transport a meteorological laboratory manned by scientists and technicians. The design and development of this unconventional craft took place at the Rhoen-Rossiten-Gesellschaft Research Institute in Munich. Its birth and growth were largely the creation and responsibility of Doctor Alexander Lippisch, a well known engineer, scientist and aircraft designer.

Dr. Lippisch brought together the best knowledge available from the sport glider and aircraft industries in Germany. By 1933 he produced a totally new aircraft that looked like an ugly duckling of the sport glider species. It had a larger fuselage than its forerunner. To give the wings strength to lift heavy loads to be transported in the fuselage, the traditional gracefully-shaped wings of the sport glider were replaced by shorter, stubbier ones, closer in appearance to those of an airplane. In actuality this craft was more like a motorless transport airplane than a sport glider in appearance. The new craft had to be towed by a powered aircraft from takeoff to within gliding range of its landing area and then released for a gradual glide to earth. As a general rule, it could not sustain its attitude by riding the air currents as could a sport glider. Its loaded weight and design committed it to a descending glide with little or no option for soaring. However, when the glider was lightly loaded many pilots found it handled so much like a sport glider that they could, on occasion, take advantage of prevailing air currents to enjoy a few minutes of soaring.

For meteorological readings at high altitudes the glider was ideal. When in free flight it was noiseless, vibrationless and free from electrical emanations usually found in airplanes that were likely to disturb sensitive instruments. The "flying laboratory" as it became known, was first towed in tests by Hanna Reitsch.

General Ernst Udet, on one occasion inspecting the flying meteorological laboratory, saw in its design and performance possible military application. He felt it might be used to supply encircled units or, perhaps, serve as a kind of modern Trojan Horse, by landing soldiers unnoticed behind an enemy's front lines.

Along with General Udet, some of the more visionary members of the Air Forces, General Jeschonnek in particular, began to press for a combat model. The design and development of the project was given a "secret" classification right at the start and was turned over to the Deutsche Forschungsanstalt Fuer Segelflug (DFS), an affiliate of the Rhoen Research Institute. An aircraft engineer, Hans Jacobs, assisted by glider pilots on the staff of the company, took the problem in hand.

The German military had experimented extensively with parachuting and had developed combat tactics for parachute airborne operations. On the other hand, no one had yet seen a combat glider, much less experimented with it. One thing the Germans realized was that landing men by glider had certain advantages over dropping them by parachute. The glider could carry a unit of men—perhaps a squad of seven to nine—and land them together ready to fight. In contrast, parachuting scattered the men into patterns 150 to 200 yards long and for this reason they had difficulty in getting assembled and lost much time in the process. If under fire while reassembling there might be heavy losses. The glider landed quickly, in small areas, and its men were ready to fight upon landing and did not have to cope with the problems of getting out of a parachute harness. Another feature that helped to sell the military on the advantages of the glider was its silence. It could be released miles from its target and probably land without detection. Rarely could a parachute operation have the surprise of a glider landing. But because there was no unanimity of viewpoints on just what the objectives of the program should be, controversy raged for some months before Jacobs' team received a clear directive.

He was to design a glider that could carry nine fully-armed soldiers, glide and dive noiselessly and land on uncultivated short fields. The Germans aimed at keeping the cost at 7,500 Deutschmarks. The price was based on the expense of landing

10 men by glider instead of by parachute. In other words, the price was equivalent to the cost of manufacturing ten parachutes

In early 1939 the strange new craft was finished. It looked very much like an enlarged light airplane without a motor. The fuselage was made of steel tube framework covered with canvas. The wings were set high and braced. The wheels, once the glider was aloft, could be jettisoned and the glider landed on a central plywood ski-like skid. It weighed 2,790 pounds and carried a cargo almost as heavy. A bench for passengers ran down the center. Hanna Reitsch was soon test-flying it near Munich.

A number of high ranking generals including Ernst Udet, the World War I fighter Ace, Von Greim, Albert Kesselring, Walter Model and Erhard Milch observed an experimental flight of the DFS 230 and were enthusiastic about its possibilities. Contracts were soon negotiated with the Gothaer Waggonfabrik, a manufacturer of railroad cars in the city of Gotha. Despite the enthusiasm of a few high-level people, the glider's failure to win broad acceptance in German military circles, worried some of the more enterprising members of the High Command. What was needed was someone to inject leadership and imagination into the project.

General Hans Jeschonnek, at the time Chief of Operations for the Luftwaffe, (later to become Chief of the General Staff) called General Student, then still a Colonel, to his office. The two were long-time friends and military associates. After some preliminaries in which he described what was being done in the glider development program, Jeschonnek, uncertain of Student's sympathy with the idea of building a transport glider, almost apologetically said, "Nobody gives a damn for the new glider. The best that could happen is if you would take it under your personal wing. Otherwise the whole damn thing will lie dormant."

This surprising disclosure was the first intimation to Student that anything like a glider transport program was in progress. He was excited by the challenge and willingly agreed. He took over the project and personally flew the glider many times to see what it could do. In his opinion, the glider was of excellent construction, with a good ratio between empty and loaded weight; moreover, it had outstanding flying characteristics. From the start he planned to use this glider not only as a medium of transport but, due to its noiselessness, as a weapon of attack. It went into production soon thereafter with his strong endorsement and he personally named it the DFS 230 "attack glider."

The usefulness of the glider from a military point of view, however, continued to be seriously debated. The chief objection came from the parachute enthusiasts who saw in it a source of unwelcome competition. As a consequence, a wide difference of opinion developed in military circles.

A second demonstration was held, this time before the Army General Staff. Ten Junker (Ju) 52's transporting paratroopers and ten gliders carrying glidermen towed behind ten more Ju 52's flew to the airfield at Stendal. There the gliders were cast off, and the paratroopers dropped. The gliders dove steeply and came to rest in close formation, discharging glidermen in units ready to fight. The parachutists, on the other hand who had the ill luck to encounter a stiff breeze—from which the gliders had actually benefited—landed widely dispersed in some cases a considerable distance from their ammunition, which had been dropped by parachute. Though this experiment could not, of course, obscure the importance of paratroopers in a future war, it at least proved conclusively that the troop-carrying glider could become a weapon of great value.

Large scale production was launched under the supervision of the Gotha works, and many different companies participated in the manufacture of the DFS 230. Because of the military's emphasis on their production, a large number of DFS's were ready for combat when World War II started. By 1943 manufacturers had delivered 1,477 to the Luftwaffe.

Assault Force "Granite"

General Student wasted no time getting Hitler's plan going. Der Fuehrer was pressing his generals to attack the West before the snows set in. Orders to launch the invasion could come at any moment and the General had to have the glider force prepared to spearhead it.

For several days after seeing Hitler he pondered about whom to place in charge of the overall operation to seize Fort Eben Emael and the three bridges. He carefully screened the officers of his airborne division and from them chose Captain S. A. Koch, a young officer from one of the regiments. The choice proved to be an excellent one.

Heiner Lange, a glider pilot, praised Koch as a sensitive, highly talented officer who had the qualities of a great artist. This was best demonstrated in the imaginative way in which he organized and prepared his forces for the attacks ahead.

Lieutenant Witzig, who was to lead the attack against the Fort, found Captain Koch a visionary who came up with incredible schemes that, coming from someone else, would have been considered mad. Those knowing Koch rarely doubted the merit of any of his ideas, wild as some of them might have sounded. He was no "yes" man. Before he accepted an order he took the time to study it. Before he agreed to carry it out he had to be convinced in his own mind that it would succeed. High on the list of the criteria an order should meet was that each man involved had a reasonable chance of coming out of the mission alive.

Assault Force Granite several weeks before the attack on Eben Emael.

The author in front of the entrance of a casemate of the Benes Line along the Czech border, 1950.

For the task of taking Fort Eben Emael and the bridges it seemed as if Koch had unlimited power and many assumed it was because he had a direct line to Adolf Hitler. General Student disclaims any such connection although he acknowledges that Hitler had a high regard for Koch from the outset. General Student's interest and responsibility for the operation, backed as he was by General Hans Jeschonnek, Chief of the General Staff of the Luftwaffe, and a veteran in sport glider flying, provided Koch with everything he needed. General Jeschonnek had great faith in the glider as a military weapon and wanted to see the operation succeed, convinced the glider was the answer to many of Germany's future military needs.

At one time Witzig, foreseeing the need for more realistic training, came to Koch with the demand for larger training areas and some concrete casemates against which practice attacks could be made.

He got Witzig a large training area near Hildesheim. There Witzig laid out boundaries of the Fort on soil closely resembling the limestone composition of the surface soil of Fort Eben Emael. There his squads simulated landing in gliders and worked out tactics and the coordination that would assure them success in the real attack.

For casemates Koch turned over to Witzig three hundred miles of the Benes line fortifications. The line lay in Sudetenland and followed the meandering Czechoslovak-German border. Its immense casemates, bristling with guns, blocked tactically important avenues an enemy might use to enter Czechoslovakia. Skillfully designed and equipped with the most advanced guns and equipment from the famed Skoda works in the city of Pilsen, and from armament factories in the Bohemian city of Brno, the Benes Line was the pride of that small nation.

To the dismay of the Czechoslovak people the Benes Line fell in 1938 without a shot being fired. The Czechoslovak Army, probably better trained for war than any in Europe, was disbanded after Munich when England and France sacrificed the Czechs for a paltry year of peace. Witzig selected a segment of the Line near Sumperk, 100 miles west of Prague, and there his men became familiar with fortifications and how to assault and destroy them.

In another instance Captain Koch was watching pilots practice glider landings on a grassy field wet with dew. The pilots found that the plywood landing skid of the DFS 230 on the wet grass caused unduly long slides before the glider came to a halt. They foresaw difficulties in stopping quickly in the limited spaces available for landings on the surface of the Fort. They were also concerned that they might have to land and stop on ice or snow should the attack be ordered during winter. To shorten the landing slide pilots wrapped barbed wire around the skid. This helped but not enough. Heiner Lange suggested that a jaw-like plow be rigged so that it could be let down and plow into the ground for more rapid deceleration.

Captain Koch snapped up the idea. Within moments he was on the telephone to the DFS research staff and presented the problem and Lange's idea to them. In turn it was given to Hans Jacobs who, the following morning had designed and built a braking device and installed it on a glider. Hanna Reitsch, the internationally known gliding and soaring champion who had some inkling of the forthcoming operation against Fort Eben Emael, soon had the glider in the air. The experiment almost proved fatal.

She was to discover on the very first test that its braking power was much greater than she had imagined. To prevent the control column from digging into her during a sudden stop, she had padded herself with a number of blankets. But when she applied the brakes the effect was so strong that she was thrown violently forward against the safety belt, the wind knocked out of her. For some minutes she was too dazed to move and finally, white as chalk, had to be helped out of the machine. Modifications were then made to the brake to reduce its plowing effect. She flew test after test, at first with an empty machine and then with full load, until finally the brake was declared satisfactory.

In 1931 this diminutive aviatrix had captured the women's world record for non-stop gliding. She had remained aloft five and a half hours. Two years later she doubled this record. Later she went on to set many more German and International records. In 1939 she attended the United States International Air Races where she performed glider acrobatics. In the mid 1930's her exploits drew Hitler's attention. Thereafter he sought her advice about the use of gliders and their technical performance, undoubtedly greatly increasing his knowledge and confidence in the glider. She tested many new glider models that were developed in Germany during the war. She piloted the huge Messerschmitt 230, 200-passenger transport glider in Troika tow behind three straining Heinkel 111 bombers. Ultimately she became a Flight Captain and a member of General Udet's staff.

Another incident illustrated the prescience of Captain Koch while a unit commander on the Russian front. As was the case with most German commanders during the war, he found himself faced with an aggressive and overwhelming Russian force. His unit was taking heavy losses and something had to be done. Stored in his unit's supply dump were barrels of chalky blue powdered limestone. This was used by German ground units to indicate their trench systems to the Stuka dive bombers. Koch ordered this powder spread during the night in a belt 20 yards in front of his trenches. Koch's troops, puzzled but obedient, did his bidding. From the time the chalk mysteriously appeared between the German and Russian trenches the superstitious Russians did not attack Koch's position.

A lover of sports cars and speed, Koch was reported to have

said that only Hermann Goering was entitled to drive cars faster than he on the magnificent new German Autobahn. Koch was decapitated on 23 October 1943, on the autobahn between Berlin and Magdeburg when his speeding roadster ran under the rear of a huge truck.

On 2 November 1939 General Student activated the "Sturmabteilung" (Storm Group) that was to have the historical mission. Its first home was in an Army Barracks in Hildesheim, a city in the foothills of the Harz mountains in Northern Germany, long an area used by the German Army for maneuvers and suited to the training needs of the Storm Group. One of the units drawn into the group was a platoon of paratrooper engineers from the 7th Airborne Division. The two officers, 73 men and eleven glider pilots of this platoon formed the nucleus of the group that was scheduled to land on Fort Eben Emael.

Most of the men had been together for at least a year. The unit had grown from a small corps of Germany's first military parachutists. Sergeant Helmut Wenzel, who was to earn fame in the forthcoming attack, was one of the men graduated in the first training class of military parachutists. When an experimental test unit of paratroopers was organized in 1938, Wenzel became its squad leader. As war loomed, and the German Army expanded, the unit grew to platoon size. In 1938 it got its first platoon leader, Lieutenant Rudolf Witzig. Witzig was 23 years old, a skilled engineer, unmarried and a dedicated professional officer. He was a first-rate choice for a soldier's job where initiative and courage were needed. No one questioned whether he was a dedicated Nazi, for no one was dispensing political plums to second-rate hangers-on at this point.

When the call for volunteers to man the Storm Group was made, there was an overwhelming response. Quickly Koch's Group recruited to its authorized strength of 11 officers and 427 men, and as it developed into a cohesive combat force, it became better known as "Storm Group Koch" after its dynamic leader. As for Witzig's platoon of parachute engineers, it was a harum-scarum group of men as most parachute volunteers usually were. Few bent willingly under harsh Prussian discipline. Many had records for minor disciplinary infractions, each was a determined individualist with a reputation for fearlessness. In all, they added up to a devil-may-care group such as had never before been collected into one unit in the German Army.

Already in training a year, the unit had served in the Polish campaign but, to the chagrin of its members, had not tasted combat. They had constructed roads, dug trenches and performed other inglorious combat-support tasks. The most they could boast of was that they had helped guard some Polish prisoners. When they returned to Germany most of them had served almost two years and were expecting to be discharged. But the discharges never came. They were told to forget their plans to get back to civilian life, to school, job or family. There was another job to be done.

On 3 November, Captain Koch had received his top-secret orders. They directed him to accomplish three tasks. First, by surprise glider landings, to capture the bridges of Vroenhoven, Veldwezelt and Canne intact. Second, to destroy with explosives the artillery and works of Fort Eben Emael and, third, to hold his positions at the bridges and the Fort until the arrival of German ground forces who were to relieve Koch's units.

Captain Koch divided the Storm Group into four forces. Lieutenant Witzig's platoon, ultimately named "Granite", was to take Fort Eben Emael. Lieutenant Schacht, commanding a 96-man glider force was given the capture of the Vroenhoven bridge as his mission. This force was named "Concrete". Lieutenant Altmann received command of the 92-man force "Steel" that was to seize the Veldwezelt bridge. A 92-man force, "Iron", commanded by Lieutenant Schaechter was assigned to take the bridge at Canne.

On 3 November General Student clamped tight secrecy on every detail of the operation. So rigid were the precautions that the attack on Fort Eben Emael and the bridges later became famous as one of the best kept secrets of the war, akin to the secrecy that cloaked the Japanese preparation to attack Pearl Harbor or that which cloaked the development of the atomic bomb by the United States.

The details were so closely guarded that most of Germany's top ranking generals were ignorant of the impending glider foray. Witzig ordered all insignia of rank removed. The men were ordered not to send mail or make telephone calls. None were allowed to go on leave or mingle and talk with soldiers of other units. Each member of Koch's unit had to sign the following statement:

> I am aware that I shall risk sentence of death should I, by intent or carelessness, make known to another person by spoken word or illustration anything concerning the base at which I am serving.

The whereabouts and activities of Witzig's platoon were cleverly concealed from all but those who had an official right to know, and by the use of a bewildering number of cover names and deceptive troop movements. The platoon was first named Flughaven Bauzug (Airport Construction Platoon). Other names followed as it moved from one training area to another, its final name becoming Sturmgruppe Granit (Assault Group Granite). Its many names, its moves, the way it was kept isolated from military and civilians alike spread an aura of mystery around the unit wherever it appeared. Its presence in any area evoked hush-hush guesses and provoked a rash of rumors as to its mission.

Training Activities

Although each man had parachuted many times, to most the glider was something of a mystery. The paratroopers did not look forward to flying in a glider. They felt much safer dropping by parachute into combat. General Student realized as did the British and Americans much later that men who were to go into combat by glider could not be simply led, sheeplike, into the glider at the last moment before the operation. There was much more to the business. The men had to learn, for example, how to get in and out of the glider, and hold their weapons and move into place with caution so that a carelessly held rifle would not poke a hole through the fuselage. One such accident in a critical place could take the fragile glider out of action as quickly as if hit by a whizzing piece of flak.

In the DFS 230 the glidermen learned to straddle the narrow central seat, one in back of the other, facing the nose of the glider. Knees and hobnailed boots pressed against gear stowed underseat or lashed to the glider walls. Everything had to be tightly secured. Hemp rope lashed heavy items to the steel framework; anything loose could be expected to rise in the air or bang against the side of the glider in the bumpy turbulence caused by the engines of the tow craft. Before lashing techniques were perfected and troops became convinced of the necessity to tie equipment down, several soldiers suffered bruises from heavy equipment tumbling through the air as gliders came to screeching halts in practice maneuvers.

From the pilot's standpoint, it was not enough to become proficient in piloting the DFS 230 without combat load. An equivalent dead weight would not give the feel of men and gear, the smell of perspiration, or the jibes to be taken as men tried to relieve their tensions enroute to a harrowing job. Thus, shortly after glider pilots had made some formation flights, Koch scheduled the squads of Witzig's group into glider flights much as Witzig had organized them for combat. At first the men had a flight or two just for the feel of it, to give them confidence in their strange new mode of transportation. Soon Witzig had them out on the runways with equipment. Each squad then had to figure out how to fit and securely tie every item in the glider. Many experiments took place. Bull sessions were frequent, usually devoted to discussion of the best ways to get the multitude of new jobs done. Safety was a prime factor and the glider pilot had to be the ultimate judge of whether the gear would change the center of gravity and thereby alter the flight characteristics, making the glider either unmanageable or dangerous to fly.

Reassured many times by ordnance experts brought to Hildesheim to teach the teams to handle the newly invented hollow charge, the men, nevertheless, treated the explosives gingerly. No one wanted 110 pounds of TNT to break loose and float in the air around his head as the glider bounded through the atmosphere.

For awhile Koch wondered if the tasks required of the glider pilots were beyond their ability. Pinpoint landings would be required to place assault troops and the heavy explosive charges close to their objectives. If the Belgians were alert, or if it took too much time to get from glider to casemate, the mission might fail.

Koch had inherited a Lieutenant Kiess and a nucleus of pilots from a glider development unit formed a year earlier in the German Air Force. As glider pilot Heiner Lange pointed out, these men had little soaring and sport glider experience. They had not developed the sensitivity and dexterity that comes from flying a sport glider in changing air currents. Of more critical significance, being accustomed to landings on prepared runways, they were consistently overshooting targets on the natural terrain used in training for the Granite operation.

Desperately seeking solutions to a problem he was not even certain could be solved, Koch called on the DFS Institute for help. It sent him two veteran glider test pilots, Kartaus and Opitz, from its staff. These pilots, quite simply, demonstrated to Koch's satisfaction that the problem lay not with the versatile DFS 230, but with the imperfect skill of the pilot. Koch prevailed on them to begin a training program for his own pilots, which they undertook. Koch, aware of their critical importance to his operation, began to take measures to have the two drafted into his staff. However, they wanted no part in landing gliders in combat. Koch agreed to release them only on the condition that they gave him a list of names of other qualified pilots. This eventually led to many a bewildered sport-glider champion receiving a polite invitation from the Luftwaffe to "volunteer" his services for a "delicate" mission. Thus it came about that men like Heiner Lange, Brautigam, Raschke, Bredenbeck and other nationally and internationally known German glider pilots became involved in the Fort Eben Emael operation.

Heiner Lange was one of the last who was unwillingly drafted into "volunteering". His case was typical. On 9 November 1939 he arrived at Hildesheim to be interviewed and checked out. As he now tells it, he found himself in a DFS 230 loaded to capacity with soldiers. In triple tow with two other gliders behind a Ju 52 he was soon proceeding down a runway in a glider to which he had been introduced about one half hour before. Moreover, he had never been towed by so huge an airplane, and he found the turbulence at ground level an entirely new sensation. It was dangerous business and his passengers were undoubtedly totally unaware that they were on Lange's maiden flight in a transport glider. He kept the glider on the runway for a long time trying to get the feel of it, meanwhile shooting

Above, a DFS 230 Attack glider. This particular glider was captured by the British in North Africa. Below, DFS 230's in single tow.

glances to right and left so as to keep a safe distance from the gliders on either side. Finally, he pulled back on the stick. The glider responded instantly, much to his surprise, and he was airborne. His experience with the sport glider proved to be enough to enable him to fly safely but it was a great strain.

He was still flying somewhat less than confidently when he had to cut away from the tow craft. He stayed in the air as long as he could to get the feel of the glider in free flight. He then landed so accurately that he stepped from the door of the glider on to the center of the cross which was his landing lark. With this accomplishment, as he said, he made the team. Gradually the professional pilots, who had little rank because they had been drafted and the old-timers "who had all the rank but little experience," as Lange put it, became a unit. But petty jealousies continued to plague the pilots and Koch never quite raised their morale to the level existing among the glidermen. Those who had been in the unit a longer time claimed the draftees couldn't salute, while Lange's friends taunted back that the others couldn't fly. The split was wide at the operational planning level and caused Koch many headaches. One contention held by Lieutenant Kiess was that gliders could not be towed at night.

Most of the glider pilot volunteers, despite their extensive experience with the sport glider in national and international events, had never seen the DFS 230, or had piloted anything larger than the two-place sport glider. Thus, they were obliged to enter into an intensive transitional training program.

Because of their previous experience with the sport glider, they went immediately to solo flights, none finding any difficulty in becoming accustomed to the large but easily handled DFS 230. Then they advanced to formation flying, which was new to many of them although about ten had had experience in "daisy chain" formation flying (one sport glider tied in succession to another). Much of the flying took place at night concealing their activities, and the darker the night, the better for the pilots since it sharpened their visual acuity, and prepared them for the kind of light they were to encounter during the operation. The Luftwaffe ultimately settled on the "chain" takeoff technique in starting formation flights. In this operation, a leading combination consisting of a Ju 52 (the tow plane) and a DFS 230, sped far down the runway and became airborne before the next combination began moving. The leaders of the operation put great stress on a "good marriage" between the airplane and glider pilots so that, by D-day, each could almost sense the other's position and anticipate his movements. By March these glider pilots could take off into the night, maneuver into formation, and when cast off from the tow plane, land on an unfamiliar field.

Pilots were trained to make pinpoint landings, and soon each one became so skilled that he could land his DFS 230 within 20 meters of an assigned target. Accordingly, on D-day the glidermen were only briefly under fire, and were able to take up their assault positions within moments.

In the meantime, Captain Koch drove his officers and men hard in preparation for ground attacks. Those who were to attack the bridges simulated assaults on bridges in Germany that resembled the ones they were to capture in Belgium. All the trainees studied the special features of pillboxes, cupolas, and concrete emplacements similar to those on the surface of the Fort. From the data obtained from German workmen who had helped to construct Fort Eben Emael, deserters, and from many picture postal cards gathered by German intelligence, the soldiers became acquainted with each type of defense installation, including embrasures, weapons and fields of fire. Each glider pilot took rigorous ground training because, when his glider skidded to a stop, he would automatically become a full-fledged participant of the assaulting force. Troops and pilots studied accurately-scaled table models of the Fort and the bridges.

From the German viewpoint there were essentially three systems in the Fort with which they would have to contend. The artillery was the largest and the most likely to slow the German ground invasion. The second was the walls of the Fort protected by machine and antitank guns. These the German ground units would have to attack should Witzig's force not be successful. The third was the antiaircraft machine guns on the surface. These were no serious threat to German ground operations in the opening stage of the invasion. However, these guns could harass low-flying Stuka bombers and they could play havoc with parachute or glider operations in the area, particularly any directed at the surface of the fort.

With typical thoroughness, the Germans set out to develop methods to cope with each system. The most important task was to destroy the artillery, more particularly the artillery that could fire to the north where General von Reichenau's armor would pass. The immense casemates and cupolas at first appeared unassailable and virtually indestructible. With long-handled pole charges it was hoped that embrasures might be ruptured or their guns blown. Small charges might be tossed into gun barrels by Witzig's crew, and plans were made accordingly. Aerial photographs and other intelligence, however, began to suggest solutions to immobilize or silence the guns.

Detailed studies of aerial photos showed that many of the emplacements had a steel observation cupola on top of them. These cupolas presumably revolved allowing their Belgian crews to observe enemy movements anywhere and report these movements to the artillery casemates which would direct heavy fire at the enemy. If these cupolas could be destroyed in some way, or their crews killed, in large measure the Fort's artillery could be neutralized. The first objective then became to blind the Fort so as to nullify the artillery. Witzig asked for and received special small explosives that could be inserted in the peep-holes of the domes, to destroy the periscopes or disable the observers.

Concurrently with the attack on these cupolas, or even before this could be started, a decision was made to destroy anti-aircraft position twenty-nine, which consisted of four twin-mounted 30 caliber machine guns, each in its own emplacement, at the south end of the Fort. If they could be silenced early in the landings, it was thought most of the gliders could bring in their loads intact.

By mid March 1940 plans for the attack had been so shaken down and refined that they remained virtually unchanged to D-day. Each squad leader had specific, detailed orders. Witzig placed several squads under a single head after landing, others operated independently. Not one defense installation on top of Fort Eben Emael was left without a party to assault it, nothing was left to chance.

In addition, the operation of the Fort could be impaired by destroying the ventilation systems that such a fortification depended on for its continued operation. How this was to be done had to await landings and a better, first-hand exploration of the surface.

In January Lieutenant Witzig introduced his men to a new explosive, the "hohlladung" or hollow charge. It had recently been developed for attacks against fortifications.

This hollow charge, also known as the shaped charge in the United States, exploited the Munroe effect, a novel discovery made in 1888 by C. E. Munroe, an American leader in the development of explosives. He found that when letters are inscribed on the base of an explosive and the charge is detonated, an exact image is engraved in a steel plate upon which the charge is exploded. The hollow charge exploited this discovery.

When exploded this causes a powerful detonation wave against the surface of the hollowed-out area. Because the detona-

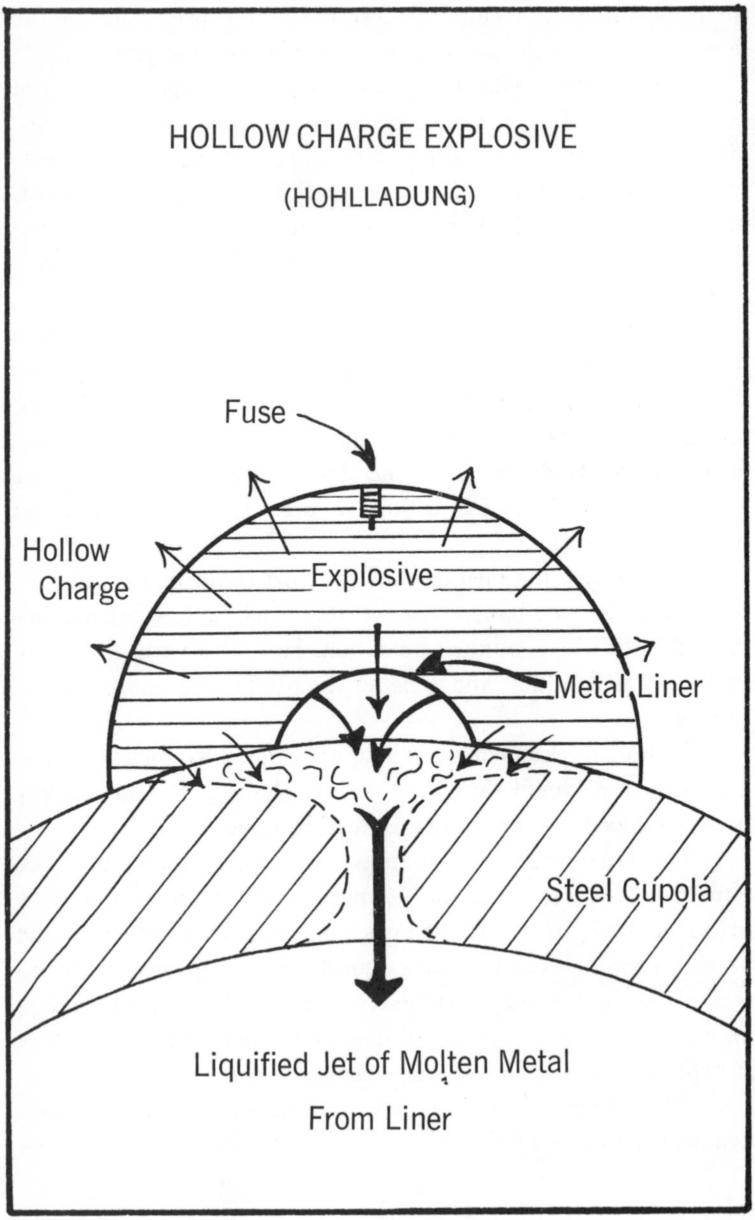

HOLLOW CHARGE EXPLOSIVE

(HOHLLADUNG)

Fuse

Hollow Charge

Explosive

Metal Liner

Steel Cupola

Liquified Jet of Molten Metal

From Liner

tion front closes the cavity, it produces in it a convergent shock wave. Extremely high pressures and temperatures result. If, in addition, the cavity is lined with a metal sheet, the liner is driven inward and extrudes as a very thin, murderous high velocity liquid jet able to melt and pierce very thick, high-grade steel.

This principle saw its realization in the American bazookas that were invented as anti-tank weapons. It also led the Germans to produce a terrifying new weapon they named the "hohlladung". It came in two sizes, a two piece 110-pounder and a bell-shaped 25-pounder. The 110-pound charge resembled the half of an apple with a top slice that could be removed. Each piece had a leather handle which permitted a soldier to carry the charge in two parts. Witzig had his men run with the 110-pounder, one half in each hand, put the halves together and explode the hollow charge at night under all conceivable conditions. He never, however, used the charge against any steel dome or emplacement even in Czechoslovakia where they had vacant useless fortifications to blow apart. The only way he allowed them to explode the device was against the surface of the ground and all they could find when it disintegrated was a shallow crater, nothing to really raise their interest or excite undue inquiry.

As Witzig pointed out, he did not want the men to know how effective the weapon actually was, as its existence was an important military secret. When one of the men would ask a question likely to divulge the real military performance of the charge, Witzig politely fended off the question. Had the men observed the effect of the charge against a casemate the secret might have leaked out. Lieutenant Witzig and his men were, as they realized later, merely the means of delivering Hitler's second and major secret weapon from the airfields to the observation and gun cupolas of Fort Eben Emael. But no one in the Granite Force, excepting Lieutenant Witzig, had the slightest idea if, indeed, the hollow charge would help destroy the Fort or not.

Some surmised it was only a gimmick that was to augment the standard explosives and flame throwers. The principle on which the hollow charge was based, the Monroe principle, was the same as that applied to a monstrous weapon to be developed at a later date—the atom bomb. The same enormous pressures unleashed by the hollow charge were later used to implode the unstable plutonium mass of the atomic bomb and cause chain reaction fissioning of the atom. It is therefore not unreasonable to assume that the hollow charge used during the attack on Eben Emael was the precursor of the world's first atomic explosion at Alamogordo in July 1945.

As a windup to their training in February the Granite force was trucked to German Sudetenland. There the 11 glider teams practiced assaulting the huge Czechoslovak casemates, using flame throwers and testing all their other weapons except for the hollow charge. Through the months of intensive training and other preparations the future participants in the exciting enterprise knew every detail of Fort Eben Emael in their sleep—except its location and name. Many made guesses and found, when the sealed orders were opened the night before D-day they had been wide of the mark.

For their task the 85 paratroopers had an enormous arsenal. In addition to rifles and machine pistols and other small arms the gliders carried twenty-eight 110-pound and the same number of 25-pound hollow charges, or five hollow charges per glider. There were lighter explosives—charges secured to the end of long poles to shove into embrasures, bangalore torpedoes to blow paths through barbed wire, flare pistols to signal aircraft, and flame throwers. In all, this totalled up to more than five tons of explosives or the equivalent of 110 pounds to each man assigned.

Fear that the secrecy of the operation might be compromised heightened in the latter part of January. It was time to transfer the gliders to their departure airfield. Until now flights had been confined largely to areas near Hildesheim, remote from prying eyes. The problem now was to get them to the departure airfield at Ostheim. The flight from Hildesheim to Ostheim was a matter of some 150 miles. However, flying all of Koch's gliders to take-off fields would certainly excite the curiosity of Germans and of strangers as the gliders flew overhead on the way to the airfields. The landing of a large number of gliders at any one airfield near Dusseldorf, a center of takeoff for all Koch's groups, would make maintaining security very difficult, especially since Dusseldorf was an area frequented by many foreigners. The slightest hint to foreigners or spies in the area of the gliders might be disastrous to the forthcoming attack. In the interests of security it was decided to truck instead of fly the gliders to the departure air-fields.

Engineers constructed large hangars at the airfields at Ostheim and Butzweilerhof near Cologne and fenced them off with barbed wire and high tension lines. Large straw mats were hung on the high fences enclosing the hangars. Guards patrolled around the clock the perimeters of the fenced off enclosures.

One bleak, cold evening military motorcycle patrols criss-crossed the area around the hangars, clearing it of curious by-standers. Huge, sealed furniture vans, after hours of driving on the highways, rumbled into the deserted airfield and through the strongly guarded gates of the enclosure. Once inside the hangars, with the doors closed, the vans discharged their loads of dis-assembled gliders and glider parts.

Luftwaffe technicians immediately started constructing the gliders under floodlights. In five days they assembled all the gliders and wedged them close together in the hangars. Like the men of the task force, the technicians were not permitted to leave the enclosure until the date of the attack.

While assembly activities were at their height, 45 military generators threw clouds of smoke over the area for several days.

Local newspapers, commenting on the incident, passed it off as an engineer-unit exercise designed to provide experience at setting off smoke screens destined to protect Dusseldorf in case of air raid.

Throughout this same period, events in Europe were working in Hitler's favor. While the Allied Armies vacillated during the "Phoney War" of 1939 and 1940, Hitler's blitzkrieg gains in Poland were consolidated, and Denmark and Norway fell to the Nazi military forces. If the Allies had attacked Germany vigorously while the Wermacht was busy with her eastern and northern ventures, they would have caught the Germans off balance and forced her to counter Allied harassment by a ground attack against Fort Eben Emael and the Maginot line. But the Allies' military myopia gave Hitler a golden opportunity. Regrouping his armies into a colossal striking force, he prepared to launch his gliders as an airborne spearhead.

5. SHARPENING THE EDGES

Days of frantic effort to get the operation in readiness began. D-day for the ground offensive was undecided. Everything depended on Hitler's mood, and no one knew when a sealed letter would come with the order: "Load up gliders and stand by for takeoff!"

Had the westward drive occurred during the previous winter, a glider attack on Fort Eben Emael would not have materialized for lack of time to organize and train Koch's force. However, Hitler decided to invade Norway and Denmark. The adventure diverted his attention from the attack on France and pressure let up on Storm Group Koch. Koch continued training his men, and as days of progressively harder training and more detailed preparations wore into weeks and then into months, the motivation of the men grew and developed into an almost irrepressible desire to go into action.

On the first of May Witzig's unit was alerted as it had been on previous occasions, and this time moved to Ostheim where the men found themselves billeted in the partially completed Flak Caserne, one of many springing up as Germany built up her military power.

Corporal M. Wilhelm Alefs, of the Seventh Squad, later recalled his feelings during those days when he realized he could be on his way into combat at any time.

"It is always better to know what is happening, but we did not. I was constantly expecting the alarm—the clanging bell in the hangar that would startle me from my bunk and into ranks, then into gliders and possibly into eternity."

"If possible for tension to increase daily, then it did, until it was hard to tell when looking at Passman, or Moelder, or Schultz or anyone else whether they were now so numbed by tenseness, were imperturbable, or just completely relaxed, content with what fate promised."

"I could not think of any other thing except the mission of my team. We knew we had to take a strong casemate, someone had given it a number, "sixteen". It was a dome-shaped object, probably made of steel. I had to carry and place a hollow charge on the casemate. I was told it could be done. I knew I would do it, at least, I guessed I could. I dreamed incessantly, woke in terror, but I would not tell my comrades, since they seemed unafraid. Every possibility as to how I was to do this and some of the other things we had to do, one by one, passed through my mind, until it seemed I had thought of many more things than I had been told by the fortification experts. I found I began to lose my fear and then I began to wait and live almost automatically until the night of 9 May, 1940."

"Everything had gone as usual that fateful day, and it was not different from many other days when we had done the same. A serene, peaceful Germany prevailed. I could see traffic along the roadways off in the distance, horse-drawn farm wagons wending their way slowly past late-blossoming plum trees, whose fragrance I wished I could inhale."

"Then it came, not as we had expected. Most of the team happened to be close by, and looked at one another knowingly. I glanced at Schulz and Hoepfner. We had been cooped up for months and had been transformed into killers. Everything we had done was in preparation for this hour! Heinemann didn't line us up like tin soldiers. That was the way most of the world thought the Germans did things. He walked from one to the other of us like a father. I was 19, Sergeant Heinemann must have ben 22, a good man. He said, 'It is tomorrow!' "

"I remember my knees trembled. Why they did, I don't know. There was no danger then—no shouting—only a great quietness and peace seemed to settle over all. Hoepfner asked some questions. I have forgotten what they were but Sergeant Heinemann only shrugged his shoulders and said, 'More instructions will come very soon.' "

"And now what? I had learned to wait. In the army, in some strange way, I found answers came finally to nagging questions I felt I had no right to ask.

"In the General Staff, without a doubt, telephone lines were red hot, but not where we were at 1930 that evening. At 2030 a few things began to happen. The guards tramping around the barbed wire were spirited off, making us feel sort of bare. I wondered what had happened to them—why shouldn't we, or couldn't we, escape now if the thought occurred? But now that I think of it, I guess the units that had their men guarding us were also alerted for the great invasion of the West, and they had orders to assemble their men from guard and other duties at once."

"Now Sergeant Heinemann called us all together. We stood around him like a soccer team around the captain just before the whistle blew. It was about 2035."

" 'Put on your gear and your insignia. Post your last letters. Keep within hearing distance.' "

"The area began to bustle with activity. At 2040 a truck drew up and men jumped over the tailgate—apparently they were Luftwaffe ground crews who were to handle the Ju 52's and attach the gliders to them. At 2045 lights around the enclosure went out. In another five minutes, a welcome sight to any soldier, the rolling kitchen, hitched to a truck, trundled up. I managed to get in line right behind Michalke to get some of the potatoes, sausages and pungent coffee. Out on the asphalt, along the runways, things were also livening up."

"Soon airplanes, many of them, roared overhead. Only their blue-spitting exhausts showed against the starlight sky. They sounded like rolling thunder."

"Awed, I listened and watched as I sipped a second and a third cup of steaming coffee, my excitement grew at this tremendous display. Out of the darkness, Ju 52's started coming in towards the hangars from various parts of the airfield, and then turned and jockeyed to position alongside the runways, finally parking one behind the other."

"A crewman placed a numbered board behind each airplane. Each glider was also to have a number. All of us on mission Granite stood out on the apron of the hangar in a trance. We had no more to do—we were ready and our weapons were in the gliders."

"At 2105 the doors of the hangars opened. A ground crew went from glider to glider and pushed them, one by one, out on to the runway, each some distance to the rear of the airplane that was to tow it. *Without a doubt this was serious business!*"

"I saw the ground crew lift the tow ropes hand over hand and inspect by flashlight every inch between glider nose and airplane tail. Mechanics went the rounds checking and pressing rope-release mechanisms in every glider and on every airplane to be certain they were operable. They tested glider tire pressure by kicking at the wheels and making sure they were attached securely."

"At 2130 Witzig gave the order, 'Load up!' I followed Sergeant Heinemann into the glider, sat down behind him, checked the gear underseat and alongside and tugged at the lashings. All lights were out. Order and firmness of purpose prevailed throughout these minutes. Everything went like clockwork. Why shouldn't it? We had done this many times before."

'Scheithauer,' the pilot called out, 'All in order?' after he had glanced back into the gloom. We all shouted, 'Jawohl!' "

"He put his head out of the glider window and shouted that he was ready for take off. But, contrary to my expectation, we did not move."

"Lieutenant Witzig's voice at the glider door announced, 'All out. Return to billets.' What happened?"

"My heart sank for a few minutes, but soon I realized this was only a temporary delay. At 2130 we got orders to reassemble at our gliders. This proved to be the last call. I learned later that sealed orders had now been opened and our job could be announced. Lieutenant Witzig read the order to us. '*Force Granite will go by glider to land and take a fort in the Belgian's defense system*. Ostheim zero hour is 0325. You have your assignments! That is all.' And that is all he said."

" 'No one will go beyond the concrete ramp of the hangar,' the sergeant ordered. Otherwise we were free. 'Break ranks.' "

"It was a curious situation. Here we were about to launch a German dream. Yet, no one spoke of Hitler, Germany, or duty. Nor was it necessary or polite. It only would have shocked us in our thoughtful mood. Our spirits did not neeed to be infused with patriotic slogans. We knew what we had to do."

"We felt like soldiers. We drifted into groups, some going to the latrine to talk without fear of being overheard. Even now we were not certain what we might discuss without fear of court martial. No feeling that this mission would fail ever entered anyone's mind. We all, I guess, brushed from our minds any thought of the destruction and death we were to cause."

"There was unyielding determination in each man's eyes. Those who are our friends, are our strong, loyal friends; those who are our enemies will find us unyielding enemies. With this feeling we could search out the devil in hell! These were my thoughts at the moment. We didn't need all the explosives. We could take the Fort by grenades and rifles, I felt so confident."

"I got out into the fresh air — there were two and a half hours yet to wait. I peered into the darkness and could barely discern the silhouette of the aircraft."

"Heinz came over, 'Do you think we will succeed?' he sort of mechanically asked."

"All I said was, 'Ja, we will surprise the hell out of them.' "

"We stood there seeking some solace, or empathy I guess. We breathed deeply the cool spring air, the wholesome perfume of spring. It was May. We stood quietly now, each deep in his own thoughts. I wondered if my mother would be proud of me tomorrow. I had no girl friend. They were for other men, not for youthful soldiers."

"At different places around us an occasional flashlight flickered cautiously. The crews of the Ju 52's lolled, smoking and murmuring, near their craft."

"Some men busily played at cards as if what they were doing was the most important thing in the world. The air was charged with tension. None of us could escape. I went to my thermos, poured a half cup of coffee, gulped it down. But not from thirst or fatigue; who could be fatigued now? I just had to occupy myself. I had to have something to do."

"It was now 0110. I went into the hangar where I sat on the corner of a table and gazed aimlessly about. Money littered a table nearby. Occasionally a knuckle knocked on the table, cards snapped, a coin jingled as the men gambled at 21, violating an old army regulation that now meant nothing to them. Where would the money be 12 hours from now, I wondered. As I looked from face to face at those seated on the floor and leaning against the walls of the hangar dozing, and then to groups of two or three men talking and joking I was struck with one fact — something powerful radiated from each man's face. How some of these men could sleep puzzled me. I had no desire for it in me. The hour set for reveille was 0145, or 45 minutes before the final assembly of each of the four glider forces."

"Some days before I had made my will. Each of us had to do this. Sergeant Heinemann helped us fill out a form that took care of important legal statements. I told Sergeant Heinemann I had nothing to will. I had left home at 16 and maybe my bicycle was still good but Anna, my sister, had it now — a small short-wave radio to listen to Berlin is in my bedroom. 'But,' Sergeant Heinemann said 'You have some savings, yes? Then you also have some pay.' "

" 'Oh, Ja, I do, but not too much!' But I did his bidding anyway. I signed a very general statement — whatever it was — leaving all to Anna who was still in middle school and wanted to be a nurse."

"Now Sergeant Heinemann came around again. He gave me a small vial. 'These are for energy.' He asked me for the will as he did every soldier. I reached into the deep front pocket of my combat jacket, drew it out and gave it to him. His eyes moved over the inscription on the face, 'This is not to be opened except in case of certain death' with my signature below, Wilhelm Alefs. He turned it over and pulled at the flap to test it. It did not open. Next, he stepped to Hoepfner."

"I looked at the vial. It was Pervitin, a stimulant to be taken when needed to prevent drowsiness. I certainly didn't need it then and simply let it drop in my pocket. I didn't see anyone take any, but I learned from some friends, joking about the business that Distelmeir, one of the glider pilots, had taken three, washing them down with coffee, and it gave him such a jolt he couldn't get to sleep for three days. It may not be true, but that is what I heard."

"I wondered again if some were afraid. I still was. Some

days after the affair was over, I was questioned if I had been afraid. I had to tell them I was."

"Our Witzig force was closely knit, very well trained now, all ready to do our work. The 85 paratroopers felt stronger than the 1,200 defenders we were to attack."

"I had been outside for awhile and again went into the hangar. Someone said, 'The time goes slow as hell, doesn't it?' "

"I heard, 'Ja, it's damned boring! I wish we were in the air now.' "

"My watch slowly ticked away the minutes — it was 0300. I sat along the wall and pulled my knees up to my head hoping to sleep. Perhaps I dozed. In a few minutes, it seemed, after I sat down, I awoke to commotion around me — someone pushed my arm and said, 'Get ready! This is it.' I got on my feet and went to my gear. Sergeant Heinemann called 'Scheithauer, Passman, Michalke, Schulz, Hoepfner, Alefs,' and each in order called 'Hier'. Then came the order from Lieutenant Witzig — 'Chiefs of groups forward, to the aircraft.' With no more ceremony Sergeant Heinemann marched Team 7 towards a dimly lighted sign in the distance that turned out to be an oil lamp illuminating a small board on a stand right under a glider wing with the number seven on it."

"Everything now was livening up. I could hear a single engine sputter, then another from elsewhere in the gloom. More and more engines caught and the noise grew in crescendo towards an ear-splitting thunder, but I did not hear its peak, I am sure, for I found myself following Heinemann into the glider. Apparently the order to load gliders had been given but was not audible above the roar of the planes."

"It was very black. I felt around and found the explosives and everything else as it should be and as I had left it five hours earlier. I patted the pockets of my jacket to feel the grenades, then the ones above to see if my machine-pistol ammunition was there, unconscious but reassuring gestures. I reached into the pocket of my inner jacket to feel the fuse and cord for the explosives."

"The glider began rocking as the pilots of the tow-planes revved the engines whose roar was muffled to us in the now tightly-closed glider. We didn't take off at once. There were many other planes and gliders to take off ahead of us and it was those I could hear power up as they went down the runway."

"Suddenly, a jerk on the glider forced me backwards. There was a jockeying and sloshing motion as the tow rope tightened and swung the glider in behind the straining plane ahead. Simultaneously, we all started the chant of the parachutists' 'The sun shines red, be ready . . . '"

"As we picked up speed, the roller coaster noise of the wheels, the slapping of the propeller winds against the canvas fuselage, drowned the singing. The wobble-wheeling tail noise ceased and I felt us level off on the two forward wheels. Then there was only the drumming of the wind and a low whistle. All else was silence. The singing had stopped. We were on our way, glider and plane, to a destiny from which we could be reasonably sure only the plane would return!"

In spite of the many months of preparation and training and detailed briefings, the takeoffs did not go well for all. The first gliders got off without incident. However, the after-action reports mentioned it took unduly long before their craft finally rose off the runway. The Ju 52, towing the glider with the Fifth Squad, once airborne, seemed tail-heavy, and labored along at only 70 to 75 miles per hour, far below ideal towing speed, for several uncomfortable minutes. It finally gained enough speed and reached normal altitude. This glider was, in all likelihood, dangerously near its maximum load, hence the sluggish performance of its tug.

Corporal Alefs, second from left, with members of Assault Force Granite at Eben Emael.

Lieutenant Rudolf Witzig, commander of the glider force, poses in Cologne on the day of his promotion to Captain, May 12, 1940.

6. WITZIG'S MISHAP

By 0335 the last glider, carrying Lieutenant Witzig and the reserve squad lifted off the runway. The takeoffs, to his knowledge had gone smoothly. He was composed if not relaxed. Months of preparation and many anxieties were behind him. He could do nothing more, at least for the next 50 minutes, until Corporal Pilz, the pilot, landed the glider on the Fort.

All were silent during the critical moments of takeoff as Pilz deftly handled the controls to get the two tons of men and equipment into the air. The darkness made the takeoff a tricky business. Pilz finally nursed the glider into the air and Witzig could feel they were climbing rapidly. The whole flight was to last only 50 minutes and Pilz had to get to 8,500 feet. It meant 45 miles steady climb from takeoff to the unhitching point just northwest of Aachen, Germany.

Corporal Pilz pointed out beacons, one after another as they came into sight, placed in Germany by Luftwaffe ground support units to mark the 45 mile route the air armada had to follow. At a crossroads near Effern a huge bonfire was the first of the beacons. At Frechen, three miles further west, a stationary blue-white beam of a searchlight pierced the blackness, marking another of the guide points. Except for these beacons the country below showed no lights. Germany was on a wartime alert and a blackout was in force. The beacons were falling behind, one by one, the men counting each loudly as they flew by, when suddenly the glider was jerked violently downward. Everyone inside stiffened with fright. Pilz saw the reason for the sudden dive whiz past. It was an airplane perilously close, overhead. The Ju 52 pilot towing Pilz' glider had suddenly seen the other airplane bearing towards his own on a collision course. He dove instictively, unable to give Pilz any warning.

Pilz reacted immediately, pressing the stick forward hard to synchronize the dive of the glider with that of the Ju 52. He could only guess at the direction of the sudden change in course. Although he had very adeptly handled the glider, the undue strain on the tow rope proved too great and it snapped. The remnant of the heavy rope lashed whip-like against the plexiglass nose. Then the churning noise caused by the turbulent slipstream changed to a low whistle. The glider was free but still in a powerful dive and nobody knew yet if it had been badly damaged by the unprecedented contortions and the lashing of the tow rope.

Corporal Pilz pulled back on the stick with increasing vigor. The glider responded beautifully. Stomachs sagged under the force caused by the pressures generated by Pilz' effort to get the glider into level flight. Pilz now swept upward to squeeze every inch of altitude from his dwindling speed and then, as his airspeed dropped dangerously low, he nudged the controls forward and leveled out. He banked to the right and began a slow descent, as slow as he could, for many decisions had to be made.

Realizing they were again safe, tension eased as the glider began to resound with, as Witzig called it, "purple" oaths irritated by their misfortune.

When Lieutenant Witzig gained control of his rage he questioned Pilz, "Can we make it to the Fort?"

"Definitely not!"

"But are you sure?"

"Certainly! I have only 3,000 feet altitude."

Would months of his work be for nothing, thought Witzig. He quickly assessed the situation. He might seek to get as far west as he could, but then he would most likely have to land in Holland and risk capture. Or, he could try to land in Germany. If he could do this there was some hope that he might be able to save the situation. He chose the latter course.

"Get back to the east side of the Rhine — try to make Ostheim," he instructed Corporal Pilz.

Pilz had his hands full. Fortunately the training and experience the glider pilots had received in night flying was to pay off. He peered through the plexiglass into the gloom searching for the beacons or for silvery bends of the Rhine river, or something he could get his bearings by. He finally turned on a compass course east as his best bet, saying to Witzig, "We are going towards Cologne now. Maybe we can make it." Then, a few seconds later he called, "There's the Rhine," and soon all were able to see it as the glider slid down slowly through space.

Corporal Pilz started to bank as he looked for some telltale mark — a fence, a row of trees, anything that would outline a good field. Talking ceased and tension rose again. Everything rested on the pilot's skill. How could Corporal Pilz tell where he was landing?

All of a sudden the men heard the thrash of weeds and foliage against the under-carriage, then the sound of heavy brushing and some rumbling as the skids found the ground.

Lieutenant Witzig ordered them out. Pilz made a hurried inspection of his glider. He found no damage. He thought they were four miles from Cologne. Witzig agreed.

"Can we get the glider out of here?" Witzig asked. Pilz took a look around. It was an unplowed field waist-high in weeds, some fences in the distance. But there were no bumps.

"Yes, sir, we can get out."

Witzig ordered Corporal Schwarz to have the men prepare the field for a takeoff. "Tear down fences, cut down trees, remove anything in the way." He told Corporal Pilz he would try to find another tow plane. He ran to a nearby village where he located the local military headquarters. A pajama-clad medical officer, ill-tempered at being aroused at such an hour, was at first unwilling to believe any part of Witzig's story or to comply with his request for a car. Finally, after much discussion Witzig convinced the officer of his identity and got the urgently needed vehicle. He sped to the Ostheim airfield. To his utter dismay it was practically deserted.

Lieutenant Witzig glanced anxiously at his watch. It was close to 0405. Ten of his squads were now gliding onto Fort Eben Emael. He went to the Operations office, told them his plight, and asked the officer on duty to find a Ju 52 or any kind of tow plane. The answer came back that Operations could get a Ju 52 from Goetersich. It would take time to warm up, more yet to reach his objective. Witzig waited, unable to do more, fearful lest history pass him by.

The remaining Ju 52's towing the gliders of Granite climbed towards the unhitching point, all unaware that the command was minus Lieutenant Witzig. Straining their eyes, in the darkness, the glidermen began to see a shifting luminous horizon ahead. Each airplane had a row of eight small lights under the tail wing, set into a V-shaped metal shade facing the rear of the aircraft. This lighting system, hidden to ground observation, nevertheless was fully visible to the glider pilot. It enabled him to maintain direction and elevation by merely making certain the lights did not disappear, which would happen if the glider pilot flew too high or too low in relation to the tow plane.

Unluckily, eight minutes after the tow rope to Witzig's glider parted, a second mishap occurred. For some reason the pilot of the Ju 52 towing Sergeant Max Maier's Second Squad, waggled the airplane's wings and blinked its tow-position lights, signaling Corporal Bredenbeck to unhitch. Although such a signal at this moment startled Bredenbeck, it was not entirely unexpected. The ride thus far had been puzzling, the plane several times acting like a bronco at the other end.

A furious Bredenbeck refused to comply with the signal. "I won't do it," Bader, one of the paratroopers, heard him say. For a brief period they flew in level flight when suddenly the Ju 52 started slipping to the left into a dive and the glider began to follow. The men, behind Bredenbeck, felt the quick change in altitude. Muscles tightened as all leaned away from the dive. "You see," Bredenbeck shouted angrily, "this is not my fault." He hit the release lever.

Post-operational debriefings of both pilots made it clear that there had been some misunderstanding about the signals. This, of course, was of little use to Bredenbeck. He had a 5,000-foot altitude to use from which to glide to the Fort, a hopeless task. Fort Eben Emael still lay 25 miles west.

The force, small to begin with, had shrunk to 70 men, 80 per cent of it combat strength. Ironically, a shot had yet to be fired. The odds against Granite had risen!

At about 0415, ten minutes earlier than scheduled, the searchlight on Vetschauer mountain northwest of Aachen, the last of the beacons, came into view. This marked the unhitching point for the gliders. Had something gone amiss on the timing of the flight?

The airplane pilots, contrary to expectations of the glider pilots, did not signal to unhitch. What was wrong?

As it worked out, the flight had an unexpectedly strong tail wind. This caused several problems to develop. The gliders were 1,500 feet too low. If they had been released at the scheduled release point, but with insufficient altitude they might have failed to glide the remaining long distance to the Fort. If, on the other hand, they were able to glide to the Fort, they would land ahead of schedule, upsetting the synchronized timing of the airborne and ground attacks. The flight commander made the decision, therefore, to continue until he reached 8,500 feet. Consequently, the armada continued into Dutch airspace for ten minutes more and then the Ju 52 pilots began releasing the gliders. The gliders thus had the altitude they needed.

There was a distinct possibility that the Dutch and Belgian military forces had been alerted by the drone of the approaching Ju 52's and antiaircraft guns would fire at the airborne force. The nagging question in many minds in the gliders and planes during that critical ten minutes was: had the enemy been alerted by the sound of the planes? If so, the element of surprise that could come from a silent approach had been lost.

The answer to the question came almost as soon as they were cut off. The Dutch antiaircraft guns around Maastricht began lighting up the sky with tracers and exploding shells.

7. L'ALERTE!

Deep in the recesses of the Fort, the red-line telephone from headquarters at Liège jangled at the elbow of the Sergeant of the Guard. He glanced at his watch as he raised the earpiece and answered, "Sergeant of the Guard." It was then 0030.

"Alert Fort Eben Emael! There are German troop movements along the border," ordered the voice abruptly.

The sergeant sought clarification, but was told that all fortresses and divisions along the frontier were being alerted. "Details will come later."

This was the third alert within the last month. Headquarters was "trigger happy" was the general opinion. The garrison of the Fort was losing its ardor under the seemingly purposeless harassment. The sergeant with almost studied indifference, carried out the order. At 0032 throaty claxons started barking throughout the vast underground network, sounding in each casemate, cupola, and in the barracks outside.

The Officer of the Day dashed from his office to the guard room. The sergeant told him the message he had received from Liège. The officer grabbed the telephone and had the operator connect him to the quarters of Major Jottrand, commander of the Fort, who lived in a small villa in the village of Eben Emael. Major Jottrand answered sleepily. The Officer of the Day excitedly gave the message of the alert being ordered. Jottrand merely grunted an inaudible something and hung up. A handsome, regular officer who had been through many alerts, he was not easily excited. Nevertheless, he was a soldier. Within ten minutes he was inside the Fort, pressing the sergeant for additional information.

Dissatisfied with the brevity of the details, he called Liège. He got little more than the Sergeant had given to him. There was German activity, but no one could guess what the Germans were up to. Thus, it was left pretty much up to Jottrand as to how far to carry the alert at this stage. He determined to take the steps according to alert plans that would put the Fort on a wartime footing, but stop short of blowing the bridge at Canne and the Lock of Lanaye, which were under his command. In addition, he held off from burning down the barracks next to the Fort.

Meanwhile the giant Fort was coming to life. Casemate crew chiefs and other non-commissioned officers in the barracks roused sleepy-eyed men. Soon, the crews marched into the Fort and off through the tunnels.

A few officers and non-commissioned officers, running, some still buttoning tunics, started filtering into the Fort from Eben Emael and other villages where they had rooms or homes. It would be almost an hour before some of the guns could be readied. They were in casemates at the ends of tunnels hundreds of yards from the entrance. Once the casemates were reached, there was much to do to ready the guns.

All appeared to proceed according to plan with one major exception. The alert plan called for the crew of cupola thirty-one to fire twenty blanks shots, each one-half minute apart. This would awaken members of the garrison in surrounding villages and alert the defenders of the bridges as well as the civilians in the communities to the fact that a military emergency existed.

It was now 0230, two hours since Liège ordered the alert, yet the warning shots had not been fired. The cupola was temporarily unmanned.

The crews did not get to it until 0330. Major Jottrand got Captain Hotermans, commander of the artillery battery, to find out what was causing the delay. He was reminded that the crew was working to clear the barracks. Jottrand gave the mission to casemate twenty-three, from where Sergeant Couclet, much earlier, had telephoned he was ready for action. Back came word from Couclet that, for some reason, he was having trouble getting the blank rounds to explode and asked for "patience."

Although Jottrand fretted about this matter, he was quite certain that more information of the whereabouts of the forward enemy units would certainly not come for some time since the Fort was 30 miles away from the threatened border. By the time the Germans made their intentions known, Jottrand's artillery crews would have had ample chance to clean the heavy, rust-preventing cosmoline grease out of the gun bores, uncrate ammunition and move it to the guns. However, he was short-handed, and this complicated the situation.

It was typical of Belgian forts that they were manned by skeleton forces, while the bulk of the garrisons lived in cantonments or towns close by. At Eben Emael particularly, this was desirable because of the design and characteristics of the Fort. Although it had generous accommodations of sleeping space, toilets, and shower facilities, there was no natural light. The catacomb-like underground maze lit only by electric lights was dank and cold in some areas, and despite a heating system, was unhealthy when lived in for long periods. Moreover, there was little for the men in the way of recreation, and boredom and morale problems were the ultimate result.

To counteract this the garrison was divided into two shifts. One was housed in the barracks outside the Fort, and was considered the duty shift. The off-duty shift lived in barracks in the village of Wonck, four miles west. This location, far from the Fort, was dictated largely by tactical considerations. The primary consideration was that the Belgians did not want all their eggs in one basket. If they were billeted too close to the Fort, a surprise aerial bombing might so decimate the troops living there that the Fort would be incapacitated for want of crews. The officers and some of the non-commissioned officers, like Sergeant Lecron and their families, roomed in the villages or owned small homes.

Fortress life had little glamor or attraction and thus most Belgian military men did not care for it. Moreover, many Belgian officers considered such an assignment a questionable mark against their records. If an artillery officer was to be concerned with his future, the horse-drawn artillery was the best troop assignment he could draw, an ironical quirk in an age of mechanization, but not an uncommon situation in the mental philosophies governing most armies of that day. It takes a long time for the conventionally minded, tradition-bound military mentality to keep pace with technological change, much less to anticipate it. The U. S. Army of that period had the same slavish adherence to the outmoded horse as an inherent part of a military system. The "horsey" brass sought assignment to cavalry and horse-drawn artillery, prevailed over by a horse-show, fox-hunt social set right to the outset of World War II. General Patton, it is recalled, wore cavalry breeches right through the war, despite the fact that his divisions never used a horse. Preference for assignments to antiaircraft or coast artillery units defending such positions as Fort Monroe in Virginia, or Corregidor in the Philippines were not choice service for American officers with ambition.

At 0307 Jottrand, who was at the entrance to the Fort checking and making the rounds to see how his men were responding to the alert, heard artillery fire from the direction of

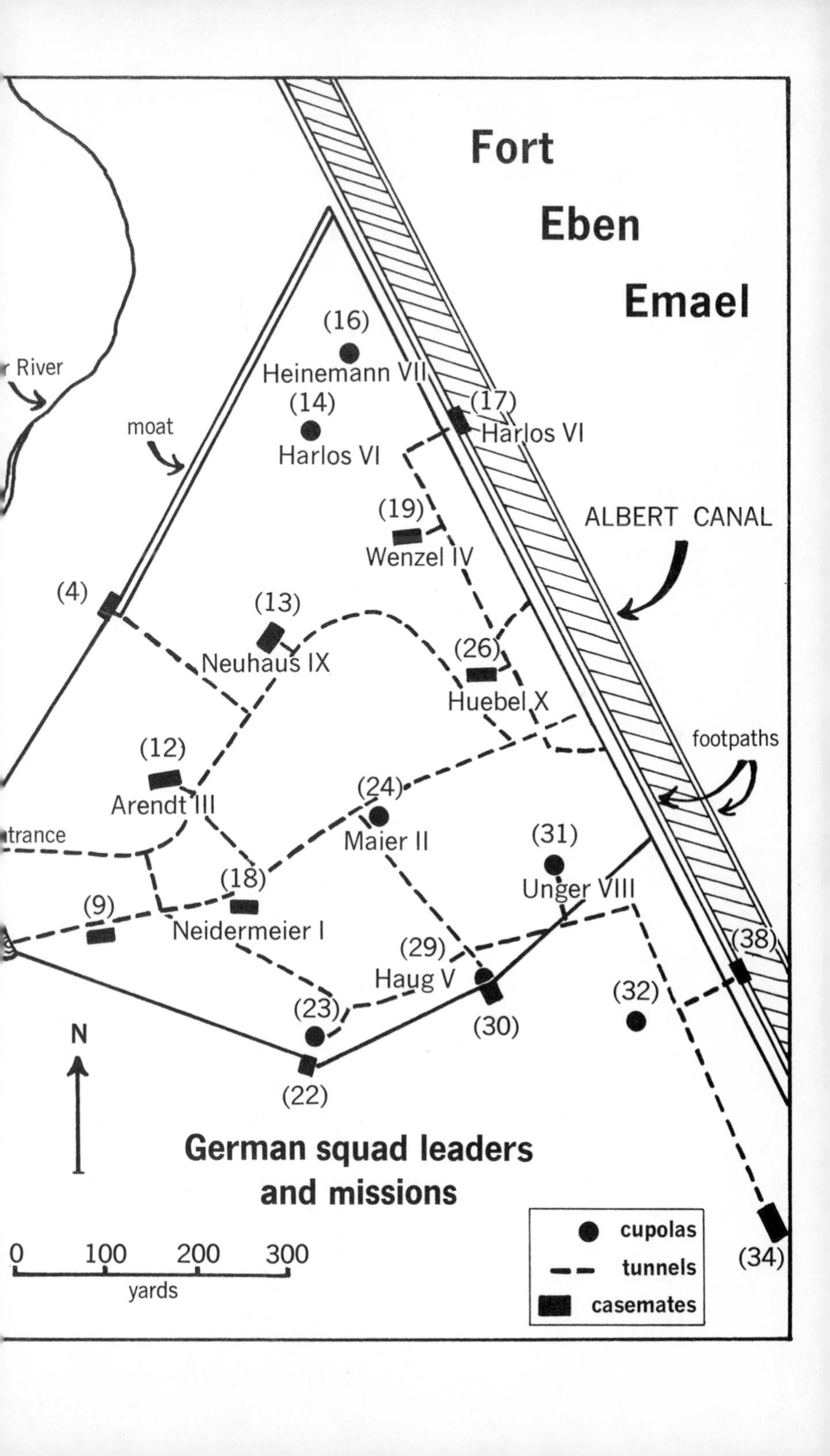

Fort
Eben
Emael
River
moat
(16)
Heinemann VII
(14)
Harlos VI
(17)
Harlos VI
(19)
Wenzel IV
ALBERT CANAL
(4)
(13)
Neuhaus IX
(26)
Huebel X
footpaths
(12)
Arendt III
(24)
Maier II
trance
(31)
Unger VIII
(18)
Neidermeier I
(9)
(29)
Haug V
(38)
(23)
(30)
(32)
(22)
N
German squad leaders
and missions
cupolas
tunnels
casemates
0
100
200
300
yards
(34)

Maastricht. This convinced Jottrand the alert was serious. He was now confronted with a weighty problem. Should he, or should he not, take the final alert measure? This concerned the disposition of the barracks adjacent to the Fort and their contents. If there was a clear and imminent danger of an attack by the enemy, then the barracks had to be emptied of bedding, kitchen equipment, refrigerators, and important records, and these items had to be transported into the interior of the Fort where they would be installed so that the Fort could withstand a prolonged seige. Once cleared, the barracks had to be blown up so no walls remained to obscure the vision of the gun crews. Moreover, they had to be emptied by dawn before enemy bombers arrived.

Because of the increasing intensity of antiaircraft fire around Maastricht, Jottrand made the decision to clear out the barracks and burn them down. He needed many men to do this. The only ones available to him were his gun crews. Orders went out by telephone to each casemate commander to send a detail of men to the barracks to commence the task. The decision was sound and cannot be criticized, although, it had unfortunate ramifications in view of its timing. Some men had only been in their positions a few minutes when they were ordered to begin the long trek back to the barracks, leaving many of the casemates and cupolas short handed, and cupola thirty-one completely unmanned.

This compounded an already bad situation. The garrison was 100 men under its authorized strength of 1,200. The Army had been slow in providing replacements for those men whose military service had terminated and who had left in recent weeks. In addition, only the night before, headquarters at Liège had lifted restrictions, that had been in effect for several weeks, against anyone being away on leave. Thus, Jottrand had authorized 100 men to take long delayed leaves. These had already left. Other men were absent because of illness.

Jottrand ordered Lieutenant Longdoz to get his antiaircraft crews to their machine gun positions on the surface of the Fort. At 0315 the Lieutenant telephoned the Command Post. He reported his men and weapons in position and that he was standing by for orders.

At 0325 the 75's of casemate twenty-three started booming the long-delayed shots to warn the countryside.

A few minutes before 0400 a report came from a Belgian outpost somewhat north and west of Canne, that a large number of airplanes, 30 to 50, were coming from the direction of Maastricht and were almost overhead at between 4,000 to 5,000 feet altitude! Belgians defending the bridge at Canne telephoned the Command Post reporting that many aircraft were flying overhead at very high altitude. Seconds later, Jottrand received a telephone plea from the mayor of Canne to be given time to get important records to safety and allow townspeople to get into shelters. Jottrand turned a deaf ear.

Hardly had he hung up when Jottrand got an odd report from another observer. "Airplanes are overhead! Their engines have stopped! They stand almost motionless in the air!"

The flood of reports, along with their mystifying nature, made it difficult for Major Jottrand to evaluate the situation accurately. What was he to do? Were these airborne objects enemy craft or not? Just what were they? Nothing from any previous war gave him the slightest precedent on which to go.

He was told by one of his staff that Vroenhoven's defenders had just asked, "An airplane has landed nearby. Do we open fire?" This unit was not under Jottrand's command, but the answer came from somewhere in the telephone network, perhaps Liège headquarters, "Yes!"

Jottrand could hear Belgian machine guns begin to chatter

from the direction of the Vroenhoven bridge. These were soon joined by more Belgian guns along the Canal as more and more of the defenders took up fire against the ghostly silhouettes descending in their midst. So astonished were some of the infantrymen in trenches along the Canal that they neglected to shoot.

The sky was clear and dawn was just breaking. A wispy haze blanketed the Fort. Major Jottrand and his officers began to see silhouettes in the distance bobbing and weaving gradually downward. What was taking place above? He could not even hazard a guess. It was a totally new phenomenon of some sort. There was absolutely no sound coming from these weird silent forms. Suddenly, Jottrand realized that the mysterious menace above was maneuvering to land on Fort Eben Emael. He ordered the bridge and locks to be blown at once.

Jottrand listened for the sound of his antiaircraft guns. But there was none. Why? He ordered Captain Hotermans to get Lieutenant Longdoz on the telephone to find the reason for the inaction.

"Why aren't you firing?" Hotermans demanded.

"I can't identify the aircraft. They have no insignia, Captain," Longdoz answered. "But they are definitely not Belgian."

The spare, wiry Captain shouted into the telephone unhesitatingly, "Well, then, shoot! God damn it, shoot!"

Unfortunately for the Belgians, by this time the gliders had broken their downward spiral. Some of them were quite out of range and others had disappeared.

What vexed Jottrand almost as much was that he did not hear the sound of explosives from the direction of the bridge and locks.

Sergeant Pirenne, in the absence of Second Lieutenant Bruyere, who had charge of the bridge at Canne and the defenses around it, hesitated to carry out his orders to blow the bridge. Bruyere had not returned from his mission of destroying the village of Canne, which the 20 alert rounds from the Fort had signaled. Pirenne hesitated to take the responsibility completely on his own shoulders since it was his first impression that the aircraft now starting to land were English as he couldn't see any swastikas. (The Germans had painted swastikas on the glider fuselage but purposely kept them so small that they were virtually indistinguishable in the early morning light).

When Jottrand found his orders were not being carried out he personally got the Sergeant on the telephone and in convincing language repeated his order. This time the Sergeant carried it out. As a result, and to Jottrand's credit, by the time the last of Schaechter's gliders had skidded in, the bridge lay folded in the bed of the Canal.

As the machine gunners sighted the gliders they fired on them, but soon all was confusion as the great bats were immediately over them, *no,* right among them! The gliders were too low now to make effective targets for guns set for high-angle fire at high-altitude targets. The best opportunity to cripple the vertical attack had been lost.

At 0425 the frightening apparitions were coming to rest on Fort Eben Emael. None of the defenders at the Fort or the bridges along the Canal had yet grasped the fact that they were the target of the world's first glider attack. Many had the impression that what they were seeing landing in their midst were disabled ememy light-reconnaissance airplanes. The defenders of the bridges to the north of Canne dashed from trenches and casemates to take the passengers prisoners only to be met by grey-clad ghosts rushing from the glider doors, machine pistols spewing death.

Private Remy, behind one of the antiaircraft machine guns, was one of the first to sight the strange forms in the sky to the north and he shouted, "Avions!" He swung his machine gun in that direction but they were out of range and he still had no order to fire. The craft kept maneuvering overhead while he and the rest of the crew at his gun stared wide-eyed. There were five, six, and then he became so confused by their criss-crossing of paths, he lost count. When he got the order to open fire he took aim and fired but his target swept past his field of vision, disappearing before he could sight it accurately.

Above the firing he heard a strange sound coming from the rear. Snapping his head around he saw a gigantic bird only yards away and five feet overhead, rushing right at him. It passed over him so close he could almost touch it and then streaked towards one of the other guns, hit the gun and swung awkwardly to a stop. Remy struggled to lower his machine gun to shoot at it as dark figures emerged. He struggled vainly, but he could not lower the gun muzzle enough. The dark figures kept coming. He reached for his pistol as something thudded behind him. He glanced back. It was a grenade!

8. OPENING THE ROAD TO DUNKERQUE

Glider Pilot Heiner Lange, a craggy giant, hunched in his seat. The Fifth Squad, who were his passengers, had the job of eliminating the antiaircraft guns. He had barely seen the dim outlines of the Fort when he was spotted by the Belgian antiaircraft crews. Their machine gun muzzles flashed angrily, shooting a cone of yellow tracers that streaked upward on all sides of his glider. "It was a display of fireworks that I did not enjoy." What made him even more uneasy was the knowledge that each tracer was followed by four non-tracer bullets and that was a "lot of ammunition being shot at me!"

The bullets tore the fabric and ricocheted off the steel tubing of the glider. The fire, if it had any advantage to Lange at all, lay in the fact that it revealed the exact location of his target.

Sergeant Haug, directly behind Lange, ducked his head behind the hulk of the 6′3″ Lange when a tracer came near but, except for Haug, few of the others realized the tight spot they were in. Evasive maneuvers were out of the question. The approach and the landing were all important now.

Lange put the glider into a steep dive as he swept south following the course of the Canal. Then he swung west for a short period until he was directly south of the machine guns. He banked abruptly on his right wing and leveled off into a nearby flat glide as he came close to the ground.

Sergeant Haug pulled the bolt of his machine pistol back and let it slam forward. The men knew they were very close. Others followed suit but the metallic closing of the bolts was barely audible above the gunfire now growing ominously louder outside.

Much to Lange's discomfort, and despite his low altitude and attempt to use the cover of the south wall as protection against the machine guns, he realized that he was not low enough, and he found himself racing right into the machine guns in his effort to hit his landing point. In a split second he would be over the south wall. Skilfully he pulled back on the controls to make a landing. He was close to touching the ground when something caught the left wing's brace, tearing at it and causing the glider to pivot and halt.

Lange threw open the door. He looked out, then down. His glider rested over a machine gun emplacement. Four terrified Belgians, hands high above their heads, looked up at him. Pistol in hand, he jumped into the pit and landed almost simultaneously with a grenade tossed in by Haug, who was unaware that Lange had planned to jump. The grenade exploded but either buried itself too deeply in the earth when it landed or detonated incompletely. Fate was kind to Lange. Neither he nor the Belgians were injured. To this day Lange does not quite forgive Haug, calling it a "Stupid act!"

Haug leaped across the emplacement, followed by the remainder of his squad. Another machine gun fired several bursts from its emplacement nearby. Two Germans moved on the gun, machine pistols ablaze. One, rashly bounding forward, tossed a grenade over the lip of the emplacement. After it exploded they dashed to the rim. They found one dead Belgian and two others dazed but unwounded.

The next twenty minutes would tell if the months of effort were to be in vain. The world's first combat airlanding assault was under way. The tactics and strategy of war from this minute were to be changed forever. The first of the enormous hollow charges would soon be exploding, the results yet to be assessed. At 0410 the gliders had all cast off, each squad to make its own contribution to the larger drama that was now unfolding.

Pilot Raschke's glider hovered quietly. A few seconds later he was able to see the Canal, then the outlines of the slumbering giant, the objective of months of preparation. "There's our casemate eighteen," Raschke announced. Sergeant Niedermeier, the leader of the squad in the glider, craned his neck. There it certainly was, a protrusion on the southern surface of the Fort. He could see no details, merely a sort of mound with a bare area in front of it. What was it really like? Would he find it constructed and armed as German military intelligence had described it? Tension among the men rose. Raschke maneuvered for a landing. What lay ahead?

The Fort began to come to life. Tracers began spewing from machine guns at the southern end. At first they seemed to be shooting aimlessly. At least they were not heading towards their glider. Then, as Raschke made a wide sweep around the southern end, a cone of tracers began probing the sky in his direction, trying to close around him. He dove in a desperate effort to keep under the stream of fire, and did manage to keep under it until he found himself safely below the southern level of the elevation of the Fort where the bullets could not get to him. His dive had been so steep he was now skimming along the ground, faster than he had ever done. His passengers were frozen like iron anticipating the outcome of the next few seconds.

As he approached the darkened mass, he and the few men forward could see antiaircraft shells exploding and tracers shooting into the sky beyond the top of the Fort. He pulled back on the controls, nosed up to get enough altitude to get over the wall, then leveled off as he swept above the crest. There to the left he saw their objective. Nosing the glider down, then flattening out into a landing position, he felt the barbed skid starting to dig in. In a fraction of a second he heard a shredding crack as the left spar of the glider wing snapped. The uncontrolled craft veered crazily, 40 degrees off from its original flight path. It was a splintered wreck but, miraculously, none within had been hurt. Raschke had done his job splendidly. Now it was up to Niedermeier's squad to carry on.

In the struggle to get out of the glider, Lieutenant Delica's canteen got caught and he blocked the door. Once loosened, all pushed through the exit. Some, impatient, had broken through the fabric and crawled out of the side. Bullets cracked, but no one was hit. Niedermeier, struggling to get the top half of a hollow charge out of the glider, became the first casualty when the charge suddenly broke free and hit his head. Stunned, hardly noticing the bruise, he ran with the top section of the 110-pound hollow charge, up the slope to where intelligence reports told him he would find the steel observation cupola. There it was, as reported, its slits facing Niedermeier. "Watching me like deadly eyes!" Niedermeier heard sounds inside. He began to screw in the fuse. Drucks now arrived, breathing hard, carrying the bottom part of the charge. Niedermeier stood off a few feet ordering Drucks to shift the charge around until it was exactly centered on the dome. Both then adjusted the upper part, set the fuse, ran down the slope and fell flat on the ground.

Belgian Sergeant Poncelet, chief of the casemate, had posted Sergeants Marchoul and David inside the observation cupola. When Marchoul first saw the mysterious figures come into his vision he was astounded, for they appeared from nowhere. The glider had evidently landed in a "dead angle" of vision or the cupola may not have been sighted towards the glider when it landed. Marchoul shouted down into the gun room that someone had appeared and now he could see only their feet

Eben Emael—May 11, 1940, the morning after the glider attack. The arrows point to gliders and the circle encloses the supply parachutes.

The crippled glider of **Sergeant** Heineman's seventh squad. In the background are the remains of a dummy cupola attacked by the Germans.

and that they had carried some large pieces of something. Before he could say more the hollow charge exploded, killing both soldiers instantly.

The blast flattened Niedermeier and Drucks against the earth. As soon as he could recover, Niedermeier struggled to his feet to get at the second turret and the machine gun position which air photos had shown to be a part of the casemate. He ran around the position searching each side, but could not find the second turret. Apparently, intelligence had erred. Niedermeier wasted no more time on the task. He noticed his left hand bleeding. His wedding ring had been pulled from his finger in the melee and had stripped the skin away. He could not recall when this happened.

Squad members Kramer and Graef set a 25-pound hollow charge against a small steel door just below the tube of the right 75-mm gun. "Fire," Niedermeier shouted, when it was properly strapped to the plate. All ran around to the side of the casemate and threw themselves flat. The explosion was murderous. The effect, as Niedermeier reported, was "Absolutely fantastic!" Only now were he and his men aware of the tremendous weapon they controlled.

The explosion blew the Belgian gunners from their gun seats, threw them against the walls of the stalls sheltering each gun and blew other members of the crew against the walls of the casemate. It killed Privates Philippe and Ferrire. It made a shambles of the interior. The 75-mm gun under which the charge had exploded had flown across the casemate and hit the back wall. Stagnant smoke grew thick. Wounded men were dragged or staggered down to the lower chamber as hastily as their condition allowed. One of the crew ran back to rescue Corporal Verbois, then turned away, hearing the death rattle ominously gurgling in the corporal's throat. Poncelet searched for Noel and Petit, who manned the telephones, but could not find them. As

Sergeant Poncelet made it down to the second floor, two more violent bursts resounded above him.

At this point Niedermeier and two Germans leaped through the breach, where the 75 had been, bounded over to the stairwell and pumped repeated machine pistol bursts into the shaft. Then they examined the interior. They came upon Verbois still breathing, but left him.

In the tunnel below, the officer in charge of the casemate ordered the emergency barriers installed to prevent the Germans from penetrating into the tunnel system. Soon the layers of steel beams and two steel doors, with sandbags between them, had been put in place. Sergeant Poncelet grimly took stock. The explosion had killed four and wounded seven, two were overcome by smoke fumes, and fires and eight received flash burns. One able-bodied man remained. Telephone operators Noel and Petit had disappeared, their fate a mystery until the next day.

Niedermeier and his squad had accomplished their mission. Raschke laid out an aircraft marking panel on the casemate surface, a signal for the Stukas that this casemate was securely in German hands. Niedermeier sent Drucks to the north point of the Fort to report his success. These details taken care of, Niedermeier, with the help of his men, searched the casemate under the glare of an electric light that had, curiously, survived the explosion. They donned masks because of the smoke. They gently carried Verbois, who was gasping for air, through the hole to the outside and layed him on the slope.

Soon the artillery that Major Jottrand had requested be fired on Fort Eben Emael by other Belgian forts, began to hit close, showering debris over the squad. One round burst close to the wounded Belgian and killed him. Niedermeier realizing that safely lay within the interior of the casemate ordered his men into it. One of them found an electricity panel. Pulling at the various levers, he somehow tripped the right combination and the air-conditioning units started. The smoke began to clear. Drucks, the runner, returned. He had made his report to Sergeant Wenzel. Lieutenant Witzig was nowhere to be found. It was about 0635. Artillery rounds kept hitting nearby. Niedermeier decided to hole up temporarily in the casemate. He had his men, one at a time, take turns at standing near the gaping opening, eyes warily scanning to warn of any Belgian counterattacks. Casemate eighteen was in German hands.

It was up to Sergeant Arendt and his Third Squad to silence casemate twelve, the last remaining threat to the German troops advancing on to Maastricht. Shortly after release from the tow plane, Supper, the squad's pilot, could see the bend of the Albert Canal where it joined the Meuse River. This was a key feature. Supper knew the Fort lay close at hand. Yes! There it was, a barely discernible huge arrowhead. Soon he could see more detail and some of the positions of the north point became visible. Twice he swept almost directly over the Fort. He could see Belgians moving at the southwest corner near the entrance. Others stood motionless gazing at him. About 30 yards above the Fort, Supper got his first burst of tracers, but this and several to follow were high. Supper nosed down hard for a second, soared up, banked on the left wing, leveled and felt the weeds below slapping the skid and fabric. The glider made a perfect landing, stopping 30 yards east of the casemate.

Arendt jumped out. "Follow me," he shouted. The men scrambled out as quickly as they could, several lugging a hollow charge. This casemate had no observation cupola, but was reported to have an exit to the surface that had to be sealed to prevent the Belgians from coming out in counterattack. All joined the search, but could not find the exit. Nor was there any sign of a Belgian inside or outside the casemate.

Arendt turned his attention to the guns. Quickly he inspected two of them. They had a heavy coat of grease on the barrels and in the tubes and apparently had never been fired. For several precious minutes he and several others juggled with a 110-pound charge, trying desperately to arrange some way to attach it to the opening of the left gun embrasure but found no way to do it. They turned their attention to the steel ball joint that held the 75-mm gun. Here seemed a promising place against which to lash the smaller 25-pound charge. They worked hurriedly and ignited the fuse and ran. Eager, however, to see what would happen, they turned around to watch while yet too close to the casemate. The explosion knocked them all flat. Recovering from the stunning effect, they ran back. A hole more than a foot square had been blown completely through the concrete. Black clouds of smoke poured out. They could hear groans inside.

When the Germans landed, Belgian Sergeant Gigon, Corporal Mathias and other enlisted men were in the casemate. There is no indication they knew the Germans were outside. The explosion created indescribable havoc. It tore the gun from its mount, catapulted it into the interior, crushing Private Borman against a ventilator unit, killing him. It continued on its rampaging course into the stairwell tumbling 20 yards to the bottom. Power failed. Eerie rays of daylight seeped through the gaping hole, wavering in the billowing dust. Moans came from unknown areas. The blast threw Engelen from his gun seat into the telephone booth across the room.

Sergeant Gigon, badly shaken, managed to locate the wounded. Gently, and with great trouble, he carried two of them to the lower level. Mathias remained in the gun chamber caring for more of the wounded, who were stretched out on the concrete floor. Propellants, stacked nearby, caught fire and burned like gigantic Roman candles, dissolving into dense smoke. The Germans began pumping bullets through the aperture where the guns had been. Ricocheting bullets hit Mathias, already severely burned.

Risking death, Sergeant Gigon pulled a gas mask over his face and reentered the gun chambers. The smoke was so thick, the fumes so lethal, that the mask soon proved useless. Gigon tore it off, crushed his handkerchief over his nose and mouth, felt blindly about a few seconds more. But his strength and breath were ebbing. Reluctantly, he turned away and groped for the stairwell.

Below he found Lieutenant Deuse marshalling a group of men for the purpose of leading them to retake the casemate. Gigon said, "Quickly, there are more wounded!" Then he sagged into the arms of gunner Brutoul.

The Germans, meanwhile, were not idle. Sergeant Arendt slid through the opening, feet first. He heard some noise but, unable to determine the direction from which it came, he held his fire. Groping along the walls with his left hand, his machine pistol cocked and ready in his right, he felt someone. He put his pistol to the man's head. The man mumbled something but Arendt could not understand what the man said. Dragging his prisoner to the light coming through the hole, he saw a be-draggled, broken-spirited young Belgian soldier. Kupsch and Stopp, two of Arendt's squad, also crawled in. They found two more Belgians, one of whom had been wounded by the burst of the machine pistol.

From deep in the recesses of the casemate Arendt heard shouts. He moved towards the sounds. It was coming from far below, echoing up the shaft from the ammunition elevator and stairs. He took a 6-pound charge, screwed in a fuse, set it and dropped the device down the shaft. The burst was so violent it flattened the Germans against the wall. The electric light in the elevator shaft went off. The voices were silenced.

Arendt decided to do a bit of exploring. Taking a prisoner

vith him he started down the steps towards the foot of the well. Ie counted 118 stairs. In three places the treads were missing. 'he Germans concluded that the Belgians had designed the tairs so that certain treads could be quickly removed. An enemy, naware treads were missing would likely fall through the open- ng and be injured or killed in the drop to the concrete floor tories below. This would slow, if not dissuade, any enemy from ursuing the defenders down the stairwells and into the interior f the Fort. He got to the bottom and found ten 60-mm shells tacked against a wall, and the barrier of steel doors, beams and andbags blocking his entry into the heart of the Fort. He climbed ack up and started to ready the casemate for any attack the elgians might launch from the outside.

Sergeant Gigon, the Chief of the casemate, regained con- ciousness some hours later. He gazed around. In a bed at his ight he saw Sergeant Poncelet, Commander of casemate ighteen. They were in Lieutenant Poli's quarters in the Fort. ergeant Poncelet ruefully shook his head as Gigon recounted his xperiences. For one and a half years Poncelet had prepared for he war. It began and ended in ten minutes, no more, no less!

Sergeant Gigon, in great pain, finally made his way to the ospital. There he saw many of his comrades with limbs in splints, andages covering gaping wounds or burned flesh, while the eared faces of others were heavy with ointments. Scorched, dis- arded clothing lay indiscriminately around the small facility. ertainly no one had anticipated this! Sergeant Gigon sobbed ncontrollably. *Only one able bodied man was left of all his crew!*

The glider of Sergeant Harlos' Sixth Squad was hit by anti- ircraft fire when it was 350 feet from the ground and coming n fast. Barbed wire in the landing path jerked the glider to a

premature stop, snapping heads forward. The Belgian wire wa
so thick around the glider that it jammed the doors. Once ou
of the glider the men had a difficult time wading through th
barbed strands. It tore their clothing and skin. Cutting an
picking their way as gingerly as enemy fire would allow, the squa
made it to the area where their objective should have been. The
could not find it. Another squad had obligingly, but in erro
blown the dome, which was a false cupola anyway. Where th
dome should have been, Sergeant Harlos found an emplacemen
perhaps for machine guns, but now unoccupied. Placing a 110
pound charge in the emplacement he blew a shaft into the eart
and the concrete sides caved into it. Harlos then set up his ma
chine guns to keep the other side of the Canal to the west unde
surveillance. As the morning wore on he broke up several Belgia
troop movements, one a column of cyclists which suffered heav
casualties from his fire.

Sergeant Wenzel's glider with the Fourth Squad came unde
fire from the antiaircraft machine guns on the Fort as it wa
landing. From within the steel dome on the top of nineteen
Wenzel's objective, Belgian Sergeants Vossen and Bataille sav
the landings begin and immediately grasped what was happening
Vossen ordered the casemate's machine gun crews to open fire
The paratroopers practically exploded from the glider to get ou
of the hail of bullets. Yet, when Wenzel ended his dash toward
the casemate and arrived at its face he found the metal door
to the machine gun ports slammed shut by the Belgians. He coul
hear the men within frantically scurrying about amid shoutin
and a babble of voices.

Climbing to the top of the casemate by way of one of it
sloping grassy sides he produced a two pound charge, set the fus

and tossed it into the small periscope opening of the observation cupola. Its explosion, he surmised, had seriously wounded the observers. However, to Wenzel's surprise, the Belgians at the guns again opened fire. It was wild and ineffective, however, without the observers to direct it.

Wenzel then assembled a 110-pound hollow charge and centered it on top of the steel cupola. To his chagrin, the charge did not go through the steel. Later investigation showed that although the jet-hot metal had not penetrated, the force of the explosion had sprung the dome so that it could not revolve.

After this explosion, stunned Belgian survivors in the murky atmosphere of the casemate below the cupola began straggling down the long stairs into the depths of the Fort. Sergeant Henrotay, the casemate chief, who had been at the Command Post of the Fort, came running to the position to take over as soon as he was told the enemy was landing. He heard the explosion and felt as he ran the blast of air, but in the maze of tunnels he was uncertain of its origin. A few yards from the casemate shaft he met the first of his disheveled, shocked crew. One of his gunners, Sergeant Diricks, passed him, his scorched skin peeling from eyelids and cheekbones. Henrotay pressed on to the base of the casemate and began the long ascent to the guns, unaware of what lay ahead.

Not satisfied that the first hollow charge had been effective Wenzel exploded a second against one of the machine gun embrasures. It caught Sergeant Henrotay midway up the stairwell and tumbled him down to the concrete floor stunning him temporarily.

When the debris stopped falling and the dust began to settle, Wenzel cautiously went to see what this third charge had done. He could not believe his eyes. For the first time he saw the tremendous power of the hollow charge. It had blown a hole through the concrete face of the casemate, leaving the steel re-

Casemate 19 attacked by Sergeant Wenzel's squad. The photo above shows the effect of a 110-pound hollow charge on the six inch thick steel observation cupola portruding above the casemate (middle photo). Bottom photo is a close up of white rectangle area (middle photo) showing the effect of the charge placed against the machine gun embrasure.

inforcing rods hanging like layers of punctured spider-webs about the hole. Wenzel and another man picked their way through the wreckage. Flashing his light about, he was overwhelmed by the carnage. Several men lay inert, covered with debris. Guns and equipment were everywhere in shambles.

A shrill ring startled him. He carefully stepped over bodies and debris and finally found the sound came from a telephone. He picked up the hand piece and listened. A man spoke but Wenzel could not understand him. Wenzel made a comment in German. The voice at the other end spoke again. Still unable to understand, Wenzel spoke back in English because, as he said, "It is a language an educated man should understand." He said, slowly, distinctly and politely, *"Here are the Germans."* He heard a gasp. It was followed by a few seconds of silence and then a woeful, *"Mon Dieu!"* Then the line went dead.

Sergeant Diricks, in severe pain, made his way towards the hospital. He encountered Commandant Van der Auwera, Major Jottrand's second in command. The sergeant described what had happened. The commandant shook his head in disbelief. Then he ran to the command post and ordered a "general attack" throughout the vast complex. It was the signal for those at the cupolas and casemates to shoot at any unidentified person and to be prepared to fire the artillery at once. A bizarre war had begun for the Belgians in the Fort.

Major Jottrand sat at his command post, his mind racing ahead, trying to gauge his opponents and their weapons, trying to anticipate their next move so as to take counter measures. He had to await developments. They came in overwhelmingly rapid succession.

On the surface Sergeant Wenzel found that the casemate he had destroyed was so well situated that he set up Granite's headquarters just behind it. His decision to stay there proved sound as events unravelled. He now had been on top of the Fort about 15 minutes, his squad's task accomplished. He ordered his men into defensive positions and went to see how other teams were doing.

Sergeant Haug had noticed that Unger's glider was in trouble. A gliderman had been hit and was lying outside under a wing. Enemy fire was heavy, most of it coming from the weather beaten, hangar-like building to the north. This building housed machinery and equipment that was used to maintain the casemate's and cupola's guns. Some of the fire may also have come from thirty-one but Haug could not be sure. He was tempted to quickly attack the enemy in the building but held off even though this might cause him to lose some men while making the attack on his assigned targets.

Haug tried but never successfully silenced twenty-three. It sat on a promontory above casemate twenty-two. His charge rocked the installation. Gun mounts were dislodged. The Belgians could no longer fire guns without time-consuming adjustments after each salvo because each recoil deranged the previous sighting. However, they could and did get off an occasional round. Lieutenant Witzig ruefully regretted that his orders had not required Haug to penetrate the interior and insure the complete destruction of the cupola.

Erroneously, Haug's squad also attacked cupola thirty. This explosion tore the Belgian observer, Furnelle, apart, going off just after he reported to his assistant, Simon, "Something appears to be landing . . . !"

It seriously wounded Simon who, at a level lower than Furnelle, did not get the full force of the explosion. The Belgian crews at the guns below remained unscathed.

Haug moved to help Unger who was having trouble neuralizing position thirty-one. But before he could go to Unger's aid he again came under fire from Belgians in the hangar. Haug, assisted by Unger's squad, attacked them. It cost the squads heavily—two killed, one seriously wounded and several injured. The area now came under fire from Belgian artillery at Luttich and to make matters worse, the 75-mm guns in cupola twenty-three came to life. The Germans in the Fort's southern reaches, weakened by losses, unnerved by the growing artillery fire, scattered for cover, each man intent on saving his life. Thus, Haug's plan to try another "heavy" on twenty-three had to be given up. Some of the men hid in a ditch between casemates twenty-three and thirty. There, occasionally catching murderous fire, they decided to jump from the wall into the moat. Perhaps they thought it the lesser of the two evils. It was not. The Belgians saw them and, from the embrasure, poured a barrage of fire kicking up stones and mortar that showered onto the Germans.

Haug and Distelmeier managed to skirt the base of casemate thirty. The fire from its guns made them take cover frequently. They finally made it to the edge of the hill above the Canal. But there, again, they were pinned down by fire that caused screeching bullets to chip the rocks around them. By 2300 the Belgians ceased their firing and the two slipped away.

Seeing the tracers ranging on the other gliders, Distelmeier, with Sergeant Unger's Eighth Squad, flew in a wide circle to avoid the fire. From a high altitude he made a breath-taking dive and leveled out just short of a crash. He dashed in from the south barely over treetops, following the course of a hollow that led to the Fort. He neared the wall well below the level of the surface of the Fort which was luckily masked from the antiaircraft machine guns firing at the other gliders. With just enough clearance to keep from hitting the wall he pulled the glider up leap-frogged the edge of the embankment overlooking the wall and skillfully pancaked to a landing 30 yards north of the wal and as many yards from his objective, casemate thirty-one.

As the glider skidded to a stop, it came under a hail of fir from the hangar. A bullet hit Meyer in the shoulder as he ran from the glider. Crouching low, Sergeant Unger, assisted by Hooge and Hierlaender, ran as fast as they could, got on top o cupola thirty-one, assembled and set a 110-pound hollow charg and ran off.

Meanwhile, Weinert placed his light machine gun just to the right of the glider and began raking the hangar. Else and Plitz maneuvered towards it under cover of the fire from the machine guns. Else managed to set off a six-pound charge at the door. Haug's squad now also turned to the hangar to give Unger's men some help. The explosion of Else's charge quietec the Belgians in the hangar.

Another of Sergeant Unger's team moved a machine gun to cover a heavy steel door thought to be an infantry exit from the gun chambers under the dome. Unger feared the Belgians could counterattack from that exit. Under cover of this gun Unger set a 25-pound charge against the door. It blew the door off its hinges, and huge chunks of concrete sagged downward into the opening completely sealing it.

Sergeant Kip, the cupola's Chief of Section, reached thirty-one at 0330, 30 minutes before Unger's glider landed. Sergeant Joiris and two other Belgians went into the turret, started the power and raised it. Joiris sat and waited, his eyes glued to the periscope lens. He saw the gliders loom into view. Astonished nevertheless he had the presence of mind to telephone Jottrand's Command Post and report, "Aircraft have landed near casemate nineteen!" He lowered the cupola into its housing. Then, moments later Unger's charge shook the whole emplacement.

Sergeant Joiris ordered the crew to prepare for action, but there was no ammunition at the guns. All shells and gunpowder were in the storage chambers in the underground system, near the foot of the ammunition lift to the guns. These rooms were locked. Keys had to be found. After much confusion, the first of the 75-mm shells was placed on one of the individual elevator cradles. The operator tripped the switch. Nothing happened. The elevator mysteriously refused to operate. Undaunted, Sergeant Hanot, at the foot of the lift, cradled several rounds in his arms and carried them up the circular steel stairs to the gun room. The crew, meanwhile, had frantically serviced the 75's and they were ready to fire. Hanot shoved a shell in the breech, another man slammed it shut and Hanot grasped the lanyard. He never pulled it. A second explosion shook the casemate, tossing Hanot to the floor, killing Biesmans and wounding Sergeant Kip.

Unger had turned his attention to the steel cupola on top. With another man he lugged a charge to the top of the cupola and set it on the surface. Both dashed a healthy distance away. It exploded. They returned to take a look. There was little external evidence that the hollow charge had done serious damage. Later investigation showed otherwise. The cupola was a sophisticated weapons system with retractable twin-mount 75-mm guns. The dome and guns raised, allowing the guns to fire through embrasures in the cylinder housing beneath the dome. The charge wrenched the guns in their stanchions and critically damaged the turret's vital control mechanism.

The explosion had penetrated the dome and daylight was seeping in. The ammunition carrying-pans of the hoists had been ripped by metal fragments and cables were sheared. Although the two guns were not visibly damaged, the damage to instruments and other serving mechanism made the installation's 75's useless.

However, a Belgian machine gun started firing through an embrasure below that covered the Fort to the west and south.

Two of Unger's men cautiously approached and managed to place a 5-pound charge under the guns. It exploded but did not seem to stop their operation. Artillery fire began to pepper the area. Unger saw someone beckoning him to move to the north. He ordered the squad to disperse. Four of them started infiltrating through the fire, crawling through the growth along the crest of the Canal bank. A shell fragment hit and killed Sergeant Unger. His next in command, Corporal Else, took over. He and two others finally reached Wenzel's command post.

At 0545, 40 minutes after the gliders appeared in periscope view, Major Jottrand decided that this casemate should be cleared and barriers set up at the foot of the stairwell.

From his location Wenzel could get a good view of many of the other positions under attack. To his west and slightly south, at the end of a long embankment, running from his bunker, lay thirteen, a machine gun casemate similar to the one Wenzel captured. He could see the glider that carried Sergeant Neuhaus in the middle of the barbed wire. Neuhaus and his men were, however, not visible.

Sergeant Neuhaus' glider got tossed about by exploding anti-aircraft shells while is was over Maastricht. The fire was ineffective. The aircraft held their formation. A few minutes later tracers from the Fort and the defenders at the bridges came whipping through the glider, ripping the fabric that covered the fuselage and wings. No vital part was hit nor were any glidermen wounded. But so many tracers had gone through the glider the men could smell the sulfurous fumes from them.

The glider landed 60 yards from thirteen. With Neuhaus in the lead, clipping the barbed wire as he went, the rest followed, loaded with gear, and raked by fire from several Belgian positions on the Fort. They managed to get behind a rise that led to the top of the casemate. It protected them while they watched the Germans attack the hangar. When the guns were silenced, Sergeant Neuhaus and several men reconnoitered the area and the casemate. He ordered his crew to assault embrasures in its southern wall from where the Belgians were firing machine guns. Schlosser moved to the flank and gave them a blast from his flamethrower. This drove the Belgians away from their weapons allowing one of the Germans to place quickly a 25-pound hollow charge over the machine gun embrasure, set the fuse and run.

The gallant Belgian gunners sensed the danger, shoved a ramrod through the gun bore and pushed the charge from the embrasure. It tumbled to the ground. Seeing what had happened the Germans scrambled to their feet and put as much distance as they could betwen themselves and the charge. After it exploded they returned and threw some grenades into an embrasure opening. These actions effectively silenced the machine guns.

Now, Neuhaus and several men set a 110-pounder against a steel door of the casemate. Returning after the explosion, they stood looking, horrified, at the awesome result. The door had been blown through, carrying with it the sides of the casemate into which it had been set. Entering, his group found several of the Belgians alive but in shock. Neuhaus organized a defense. He put his light machine gun inside the casemate at one of the embrasures and aimed it to the west. He placed the remainder of his men outside along the east slope. His main task completed, Neuhaus sent a runner to find Lieutenant Witzig to report that his mission was finished and he was awaiting further instructions.

From then on until about 1300 things remained fairly quiet at this location. The Belgian artillery then began ranging in.

From another direction to the southeast Wenzel could see Sergeant Huebel's undamaged glider. Presumably Huebel's Tenth Squad was nearby in reserve awaiting orders.

Huebel's glider encountered heavy fire soon after release and was hit many times, however, no one was wounded and it landed smoothly. The glidermen ran to cover in the brush close by while Juergensen, the runner, went to the north point to report and await instructions. Soon Juergensen saw someone motioning about 40 yards north. He sped in that direction and found it to be Sergeant Wenzel. Wenzel gave Juergensen a friendly clap on the back. Juergensen asked for Witzig. The Sergeant told Juergensen there was no sign of Lieutenant Witzig nor of Max Maier's Squad.

"I want you to take a message to Sergeant Huebel," Wenzel said. "Tell him to take over Max's mission and attack twenty-six. Do it quickly!

"Yes, sir," Juergensen said and unexpectedly saluted Wenzel. The Sergeant smiled wryly. Juergensen returned to Huebel and gave him the sketchy order. It was all Huebel needed. He was ready for this, having studied the mission of every squad before the attack as if it were to be his own.

The casemate was just in front of him, no more than 40 yards away. Huebel, accompanied by Juergensen, carried a 25-pound charge to the observation dome, centered it, ignited the fuse and ran. The Belgian fire from the position stopped with the explosion. It was now 0450.

Fortunately for the Belgian defense, because the glider carrying Maier's Number Two Squad was accidentally cast off, cupola twenty-four, housing the 120-mm howitzers, the Fort's most powerful punch, had a reprieve from the fate of its companion installations. There, however, events took a strange twist. In rapt fascination the observer at the telescope saw gliders skid in and men scramble out. He reported this at 0430.

Sergeant Cremers, the gun crew chief, got orders to fire his 120's at the Fort's entrance where the Germans, now out in the open going about the destruction of casemate three, made ideal targets.

"Deflection 75 mils! Range 200 yards! Fragmentation! Fire when ready!" Cremers ordered. The crews serving the guns went into action obediently.

Five minutes, six . . . fifteen minutes passed. The Command Post waited in vain for the impact from the heavies and for confirmation from the cupola that firing had started. What was amiss?

The Command Post was finally informed by a cursing Cremers that something had gone wrong! Crowbars used to open boxes of critical parts had disappeared from their pegs where they had hung just the night before! The men broke open the boxes with bare hands, knives and hammer claws. Finally, some ammunition was uncrated and placed on the hoists. Then Cremers got the disconcerting message, "The hoists will not operate!"

"Hand carry it up!" Cremers shouted down into the shaft. "Vite! (Hurry)." Two men, panting from the long ascent, each cradling one of the heavy rounds, soon appeared. They passed the ammunition to the crews who placed the shells onto the blocks. Another of the crew pressed the switch to power the automatic rammers that seat the shells firmly in the gun chambers. They did not budge. He pounded the switch. The armature whirred, but nothing moved.

Just 14 hours earlier, the conscientious Cremers had made his team go through several complete drills. At that time, everything, machinery and all, had operated without a hitch. The question as to whether treachery was at the base of the failures remains unsolved. As recently as 1969, in one of my visits to the Fort I was in the casemate where a veteran and now a caretaker of the Fort described the grim events. His voice carried a note of bitterness. I remarked that it was rumored that there may have ben treachery behind these ocurrences. He shrugged his shoulders and laconically said, "peut-etre." (perhaps).

While this debacle was transpiring under the dome, Heiner Lange, his Belgian prisoners assembled before him, marched towards the north point of the Fort to turn them over to Granite Headquarters. The Belgians thoroughly cowed, complained of gnawing hunger. Lange overheard one short, particularly sad looking Belgian. Lange reached into his own jacket, took out his chocolate ration and gave it to the soldier. The Belgians, hardly yet recovered from the fright of the glider landings, terrified by their captors, found the kindness of this giant guarding them completely unexpected.

Several times artillery fire caused the group to hit the ground. The Belgians made no attempt to escape. Their course took them close to the 120-mm gun cupola. Sergeant Cremers saw their approach through the periscope. He aimed his guns towards the group but because of the problems encountered within could not fire at it, nor did he desire to do so since all except Lange were Belgians.

Fragments of an exploding Belgian artillery shell hit Lange wounding him in eight places. He was conscious but in great pain. The 120's kept circling periodically and every time they pointed towards him they stopped for a few seconds. Wounded though he was, he was even more concerned that on one of their stops he would be blown to bits by a round from one of the enormous guns.

Painfully, he got up, staggered back to his glider and got one of the 110-pound charges. Although in agony from his wounds he managed to carry the heavy load back to the dome, ut it on top and, as fast as he could, he got as far away as he ould. It was not far enough. The concussion from the explosion hattered his eardrums. He is now almost deaf.

Lange's problems were not yet over. Back on his feet, he nd the Belgians were about to start out again when, suddenly, Grechza, one of Haug's men, appeared, gloriously drunk. Before ake off he had spiked his canteen of water with a healthy neasure of rum. Grechza staggered towards the lead Belgian and pointed his pistol menacingly. Lange raised his own and warned Grechza he would kill him if he so much as touched one Belgian. Grechza turned away and, in less jovial mood, went to the 20-mm gun cupola while Lange, with his prisoners, limped lowly to the north. Arriving at Wenzel's Command Post, the Belgians fixed a bed for Lange on the ground under the trees n the north point and did what they could to ease his pain.

At the 120-mm cupola Grechza playfully straddled one of he guns of the revolving turret which swung around carousel-ike while he kept his legs tightly wrapped around the gun so he vould not be slung off. Wenzel appeared. He was not in a jocular nood. He pointed his pistol at Grechza and ordered him off. Wenzel then threw charges in each gun barrel. The explosion hrew men in every direction in the limited confines of the in-erior, some tumbling through the stairwell down to the second evel. Flames from the explosion seared many. Sergeant Cremers herded all below and hastily erected the barrier of steel doors, teel beams and sand bags.

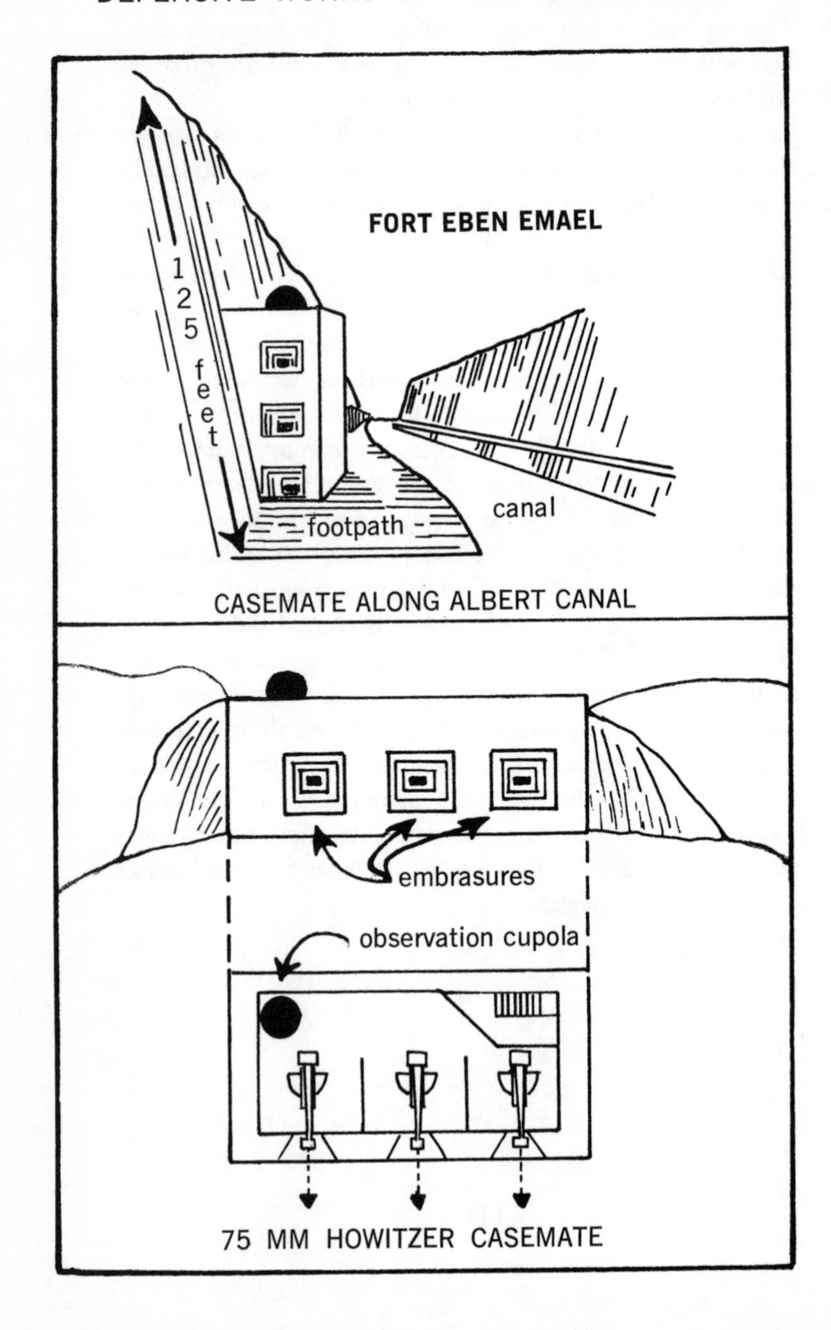
DEFENSIVE WORKS OF FORT EBEN EMAEL
FORT EBEN EMAEL
125 feet
canal
footpath
CASEMATE ALONG ALBERT CANAL
embrasures
observation cupola
75 MM HOWITZER CASEMATE

9. WHERE IS WITZIG?

By 0630 the tumultuous action of the first 15 minutes had subsided and except for an occasional artillery shell exploding all was relatively quiet on the surface of the Fort where the glidermen dominated the situation. However, they were totally unaware of what Jottrand was up to in the tunnels below. The situation could reverse itself at any moment should the Belgians pour from any of the exits and counterattack.

In the first 15 minutes of action the Belgian defenders had killed two of the Germans, wounded 12, eight seriously, four slightly. The four doggedly refused to leave their teams for the sanctuary of the woods in the north triangle of the Fort's surface where a makeshift aid station had been set up. Sixty-two German glidermen sat on top of a fort seething with enemy soldiers, isolated by miles from the Wehrmacht's blitzkrieging columns making their way across Holland. According to the German plan "Yellow", advancing infantry of the 4th Armored Division were to be at the walls of the Fort four hours after the gliders landed to relieve Witzig's force. Thereafter, if the Fort had not yet surrendered, the task of assuring the Fort's capture was to be the problem of the Division.

Except for the southeastern part of the Fort where for some unknown reason the hollow charges had not been completely effective, the glidermen were in control. The main task now was to keep the Belgians from recapturing the surface installations in the next several hours before the forward units of the 4th Division got to the walls. It was essential to keep the Belgians underground. Any major Belgian sally on to the surface of the Fort could easily lead to the undoing of what the Germans had accomplished. The glidermen had a good tactical position on the high ground at the north point but they were thinly spread. Only 40 of them were near at hand. Others were in casemates for protection against Belgian artillery fire from the south of the Fort.

Gilg, one of the radiomen, came running to Wenzel. "Where do I put the radio? Where is your Headquarters?"

"Ask Witzig," Wenzel shouted, still preoccupied with his own problems.

About this time a breathless runner arrived to tell Wenzel that Unger had been killed and that the second in command, Corporal Else, was having trouble subduing the 75's in position thirty-one. Wenzel asked the runner if he had seen any of Max Maier's Second Squad. The runner shook his head.

"Tell Witzig that. Ask him to send Schwarz's Squad to help Else," Wenzel told the runner. The runner sped out to find the Lieutenant but returned, quite perplexed. "No Witzig," he told Wenzel. He could not locate Witzig nor had any of the paratroopers any idea where their commander might be. What was equally puzzling was that none of the men of Schwarz's Reserve Squad in Witzig's glider could be found.

Gilg, the radioman, reappeared, also with the message—"We can't locate Witzig!" Wenzel stood nonplussed. Then it began to dawn on him that some mishap had undoubtedly occurred. Lieutenant Delica was next in line for command, being the only other German officer with the Granite force. Wenzel could not locate Delica. In any case Delica's glider had landed 500 yards to the south, and from the amount of firing he could hear coming from that direction Wenzel was certain that Niedermeier's Squad, with whom Delica had landed, was having trouble.

Wenzel ordered the radioman to a good location near at hand and told him to get radio contact with the Iron detachment where headquarters for Task Force Koch should be. Next, he ordered two of his men to go with Else's runner. In a few minutes the radioman came back to Wenzel saying he had Koch's headquarters.

Tell them, "Wenzel captured his casemate and that only a few of the enemy works are still operative." Wenzel was rapidly assuming command of the operation. No one questioned Wenzel's taking command. Lieutenant Delica was in a casemate to the south under intense Belgian artillery fire. He was an air force communications officer who was to call in German Air Force dive bombers should the paratroopers need assistance. Delica's talents certainly were not in the area of infantry combat.

Witzig later remarked, "The opportunity for Delica to command was there but he chose not to seize it. It was there for Wenzel who was prepared to take command. Wenzel jokingly stated that "The officers had trained all of the men so well that the officers were expendable."

Wenzel radioed for Stukas. In 20 minutes several flights were overhead. They attacked the 120-mm guns and the casemate at the Fort's entrance. Following another radio call to Task Force Koch, two HE III aircraft swept over the Fort at 600 feet and parachutes carrying containers of ammunition billowed out. This gave Wenzel another problem. The HE III's had dropped the supplies on target but the area was under heavy Belgian fire. To conserve his men, Wenzel went over to where Heiner Lange was lying on the ground attended by his Belgian prisoners. Wenzel ordered the Belgians to collect the supply containers. Lange, familiar with French, translated for Wenzel. The Belgians dutifully complied and Wenzel collected the supplies nearby.

It was about this time that one of the Germans shouted while pointing his finger to the east, *"Siehe oben!"* (Look up!) Those who were close enough to hear squinted into the bright sky. A glider, in swallow-like convolutions, was descending over the Fort. No reinforcements had been promised. It was a DFS 230!

One by one the Germans looked upward to follow its venturesome descent. They forgot all about guarding the Belgian prisoners who also watched with fascination. Did the occupants know what lay below—friend or enemy? Certainly this was a daring man who, in one glider, might be risking certain capture, if not death.

But it seemed that luck was with its crew. It drew no anti-aircraft fire. It landed near casemate nineteen where Sergeant Wenzel had set up his headquarters. Wenzel and several others came towards it but before they could reach it, they stopped dumbfounded as Lieutenant Witzig sprang out.

The rejoicing near casemate nineteen was spontaneous but cut short by the business-like Witzig. Wenzel quickly briefed his Lieutenant. The paratroopers went about their jobs with renewed vigor. With Witzig's arrival their spirits were infused with a new life.

Witzig had been extremely lucky. Everything had clicked in his efforts to get to the Fort. Sergeant-Pilot Krutsch flew a Ju 52 in to Ostheim. He kept his motors revved up, took on Witzig with no preliminaries or questions, and flew off towards Duren in search of the white kite-like speck in some field somewhere that was Witzig's glider. Fortunately, the area was well known to Krutsch and soon they spotted the glider, its passengers waving wildly below. Due to excellent forethought, Krutsch had scrounged a landing gear which the glidermen, with the help of three peasant onlookers, attached to the glider after it had been lifted off the skids.

In minutes they were trundling with increasing speed over

the field and into the air, following Witzig's clipped orders, "Direction west. Try to reach 6,000 feet by the time you get to Aix-la-Chapelle, and then cut us off over the border". Gaping, astounded peasants watched the glider until it evaporated into the morning haze.

By the time Witzig arrived at the Fort, Granite had all but accomplished its mission. The dirty part remained—entering the recesses through the various openings, checkmating Belgian counter thrusts, and keeping the garrison holed up until ground forces joined them. There was no certainty that the last mission could be effectively implemented. The Belgians did not yet know they had been roundly defeated and they had plenty of fighting spirit left.

By noon the German relief had not yet appeared. Dutch and Belgian resistance had slowed the German push across Holland. The bridge at Canne had been blown before the glider force, Iron, could take it, and hope for early help from the direction of Maastricht was not forthcoming. The glidermen were in a tough spot.

Those at the north point were widely separated from some of the other Germans. Nevertheless, because of the sound of sporadic fire they were aware that Germans were alive and unceasingly active, particularly to the southwest where Arendt was stationed.

When Arendt had disabled his casemate, he then sent Merz to destroy casemate ten. It was not certain what this installation was from the study of the air photos. It was a high, round-topped concrete object. Merz found it was the air-conditioning outlet. He blew the grill off a ventilator and tossed in a 6-pound charge. Arendt soon found the men of his casemate choking on the fumes.

Arendt decided to do some exploring. Leaving Stopp and Kupsch in the casemate, he took Merz and Mueller on the 118-stair journey down to the bottom of the shaft. Their lights flashing eerily through a murky haze, they found the latrine and a 105-mm cannon tube, but nothing else. They peered into the tunnel that led to the casemate. They discovered a huge steel door. Trying the door they saw a wall of steel beams sealing them off from further exploration. Returning to the casemate again, they noticed the air had cleared of smoke.

Belgian artillery fire that had been falling on the casemate and had discouraged any attempt of the Germans to go outside now had let up, and Arendt moved his squad out into the sun. They moved west, searching the woods for Belgians, found none, but did see some unoccupied trenches. They went back to the casemate and then, in bordom, decided to attack casemate four in the valley below. Arendt took the lead, followed by Kupsch and Stopp, each carrying half of the 110-pound charge. Approaching Indian-style, taking cover behind fences and brush, they got to within 30 yards of it. Arendt noticed the casemate had an observation cupola. He decided he could get on the surface and on to the cupola but it would take some strenuous leaps—the casemate was high off the ground but had stepped surfaces that could be used to get to the top. With powerful jumps he got to the top—the others, carrying the charge, followed step by step after him. He centered his charge, screwed in the fuse, totally unaware that a Belgian patrol, not 25 yards distant, watched his every move. Arendt ignited the fuse, jumped to the ground and ran. He did not return to see what damage the explosion had caused.

About a quarter of an hour later, back at the casemate again, Arendt lay on the turf thinking of what mischief to do next. The others of his squad were inside. Suddenly, he froze. There to his left, not 35 yards away, a 10-man Belgian patrol came into view moving towards the casemate Neuhaus had captured. The Belgians did not look in his direction. He doesn't remember what transpired except that he must have virtually sprung from his position through the hole in the casemate and into Stopp's arms. Had the Belgians seen him he could have been killed on the spot. Merz then came cautiously to the opening and fired. The patrol had disappeared. However, soon Belgian machine gun fire began hitting the casemate.

At 1500, now somewhat rested and his squad back together, Sergeant Arendt decided to blow the stairwell. He found the Belgians too active in the area. There was a distinct possibility he might be forced to leave the casemate and withdraw to the north. He wanted to leave nothing the Belgians could use. He ordered his men to move out his explosives and gear, readying the casemate for the explosion.

Because he was in such a "hot" position, Arendt sent Merz to Lieutenant Witzig to get reinforcements. He wanted to occupy the trenches he had discovered earlier near the southern end of the Fort and thereby prevent the Belgians from mounting on to the surface of the Fort. Soon Lieutenant Witzig arrived to observe the situation for himself. Witzig, satisfied with the tactical soundness of Arendt's suggestion, sent parts of two squads. Soon some of them arrived. Before he could position them in the trenches, Arendt received a report that there were suspicious movements near the south end of the Fort. He ordered his machine gun and several men into position on top and on the embankment of the casemate facing them to the south. There they could see Belgians gradually build a line of skirmishers that soon began to advance, firing as they came. The Belgians were aggressive and almost got up to the casemate. Merz, the machine gunner, was hit in the arm by a grenade fragment. Arendt decided to counterattack and started calling to various members but found they had taken to their heels. Fortunately for the Germans, the Belgians, under Lieutenant De Sloovere, by now out of grenades and carbine ammunition were forced to break contact at this critical moment, leaving the field to the Germans.

Arendt, Schwarz and the wounded Merz got back into the casemate. The Belgian attack had temporarily diverted Arendt from blowing the stairwell. Soon a German voice called. It was Wenzel.

Witzig had ordered Wenzel to take his squad and clear stray Belgians from the woods along the northwest part of the Fort's surface. Wenzel moved out and quickly came under violent fire, making it impossible to advance with just five men. Witzig mustered all the men he could spare, turned them over to Wenzel and ordered him back.

Wenzel moved out again but now a weird stillness prevailed. The Belgians had disappeared. Cautiously, since he did not know the area, his force moved southward until it reached casemate twelve where he found Arendt.

Arendt told Wenzel to get into the casemate quickly because it was dangerous outside.

"Nonsense," said Wenzel. "There's no enemy around. Get out and see for yourself."

Arendt, without giving vent to his misgivings, moved his men outside. Hardly had he done so when a hail of bullets met him killing one man instantly. Belgian fire kept hitting the casemate face which made it impossible to get back inside. They all then ran behind the casemate which shielded them from the Belgian fire. Arendt put his men into defensive positions. Wenzel shouted that he would go to Niedermeier for assistance. Just as he finished speaking, he cried, "I'm wounded—my head." and he blacked out.

Belgian small arms fire increased. Panic struck the Germans. They could not spot the enemy. Artillery shells started bursting among the Germans. Soon other paratroopers arrived to bolster the defense. Someone shouted, "Wenzel is dead!"

Wenzel shouted back emphatically, "I'm not dead! Just bring some bandages." Kramer got to Wenzel. Wenzel's helmet had a hole through it. The bullet had pierced Wenzel's head at the scalp line. Blood poured down his face and clothing. Kramer pulled Wenzel back into the casemate and bandaged the wound. Soon several other men scrambled into the casemate. Arendt dove through the opening, didn't make it completely, and was pulled the rest of the way by Stopp. Schulz found the fire on the entrance so intense he decided to try to make it to Niedermeier's casemate.

Once inside, Arendt and his men dared not get near the opening for fear of being hit as they went to the left 75-mm gun. Arendt motioned to one of several Belgians he had taken prisoner during the morning. Earlier, during the quieter hours he had had the same man explain the operation of the guns. With one of his Squad cautiously looking out of the opening, he gave Arendt the direction to swing the 75-mm gun. Arendt then started pumping shells as fast as he could load the piece. His efforts proved successful for soon the Belgian fire started to dwindle.

When the Belgian fire stopped, Wenzel and others fled to the north. Arendt and his men huddled in the casemate. They had had enough for the time being.

View of southern part of Eben Emael showing casemate 22 in foreground. Above this are anti aircraft positions, the repair hanger, and in the top left of photo, the 120mm gun cupola 24. At top right is casemate 26. In the right center of the picture are two gliders, probably those of squads five and eight.

10. THE DEFENDERS TAKE STOCK

Close to 0900 Commander Van der Auwera issued orders to many of the gun crew chiefs to retake their casemates and cupolas and repair their weapons. Sergeant Cremers, complying, found the turret of his 120's essentially as he had left it and called for a technician to repair the small amount of damage. By 0900 the 120's were operable. Van der Auwera passed this word to the Command Post. Lieutenant Dehousse, firing officer for these guns, waited for orders to fire at the bridge at Vroenhoven, which according to the Belgian artillery fire plans, was the primary target of the 120's.

Orders did not come. The Belgian situation near the bridge was unclear and Liège would not authorize Jottrand to fire nor could Dehousse get Jottrand to take independent action. Cremers pleaded with Dehousse. Dehousse did not budge. He had to have orders. At 1030, after one and a half hours of criminally dangerous inaction, the long awaited order came. Cremers fired the 120 on his left. A split second later the tube of the other gun exploded. Wenzel had tossed a charge into it from the outside. The air grew suffocating. The crew hastened to the lower level to escape the fumes. In ten minutes Dehousse got back into the cupola and checked the guns. He found them unsafe to fire and reported this to Jottrand.

The Commandant responded, "If you can replace the gun, fire on Maastricht, Lanaeken, the Canal and thirty-one". The order Dehousse needed two hours earlier had come too late. Struggle as the crews might, they never unjammed the breeches. These enormous guns never got to serve the Belgian cause. German advance elements were now pouring over the bridge at Vroenhoven, an event that these guns could have prevented. Ironically, the crew took turns at the cupola's observation ports, firing a carbine at the occasional German who fleetingly appeared in view. It was the only workable weapon left inside the dome!

At 0535 Stukas in V formation buzzed the Fort, their mission to dive bomb and destroy Belgian casemates and cupolas. Although they searched below for signals from the glidermen for help, they found none. Every vital Belgian installation lay bottled up, each labeled with a swastika, a signal it had fallen. The Stukas wove patterns high overhead for several minutes confirming the situation, and then broke away searching for targets of opportunity, their secondary mission. They dropped bombs on the village of Eben Emael and the entrance to the Fort. Peasants who had moved into bomb shelters that were dug deeply into a hill near the Fort survived. However, some of the elderly chose to remain and brave the attacks, seeking protection in cellars. Bombs killed 36 and wounded many more.

Shortly after the first of the blockbusters from the Stukas began to fall, Sergeant Lecron, a chief of one of the casemates, dashed from the entrance of the Fort to his home just outside. He had left his wife Marie there but three hours earlier frantic at his having to leave.

She had awakened to the commotion of men from the nearby barracks responding to the alert. Something about this alert that made it seem more serious, but she could not tell exactly what it was. Lecron slept on. She did not want to awaken him, there would be time enough for his duties. She snuggled closer to him. This barely brought him out of his sleep. Then she heard the dreaded sound—boots clomping up the hardened dirt pathway to the door and, although she expected it, a startling bang sounded on the weathered door and a voice shouted "Alert!"

Lecron grumbled and slowly began to stir. Soon he had his feet over the edge of the bed listening intently. Marie now sat up and got beside him, throwing her arms around his broad shoulders. Without words, he drew her arms away and groping about, slowly put on his uniform piece by piece. He sensed that she was watching him in the darkness. He could hear muffled sobs. Gruffly, to hide his own emotions, he said: "another practice alert," but his words were not convincing.

Dressed, he kissed her, went to the three children and, in awkward fondness, leaned over and touched their lips and stroked their heads affectionately with his gnarled peasant hand. At the door he put his arms around Marie and then left. It was not a different goodbye in a physical way, but is was different. The sound of his boots on the hard ground mingled with the tramp of the others as they adanced closer and closer to the Fort. He had only 100 yards to go to reach the entrance.

Lecron, deep in the recesses of the Fort when the Stukas attacked, nevertheless could sense the location of the explosions. The bombs were falling around the entrance.

Lecron, fearful for the safety of his family sought permission to remove his family—and take them inside the Fort. Chaplain Meesen pleaded his case before Commandant Van der Auwera who shrugged, "Allez!" As soon as Lecron left the entrance he saw that almost half of his cottage had vanished. He ran to it, frantically tore at the rubble and came first on Marie, then on two of the children, all dead.

The smallest daughter was crying but was miraculously unhurt. He did not dally, but wrapped the infant in his jacket and dashed back to the Fort and the safety of its interior. He took the baby to the dispensary. An armorer bent some sheet metal into a crude cradle and there she remained, occasionally visited by her father when he could take a few minutes away from his casemate.

Chaplain Meesen, administering to the wounded and dying, had free rein to move to any part of the Fort and became a first-hand witness to many of the events. Shortly after some heavy explosions he heard the gloomy news that twelve had been knocked out. Soon the wounded from the casemate, some walking, others carried, filtered into the hospital. They were lacerated, blackened from smoke, burned and many were covered with blood. None could guess what fiendish device caused the explosions. Several told him there might still be some seriously wounded in the stricken casemate, Verbois among them. He knew Verbois, a serious lad and a Catholic, to whom he had given communion many times.

Chaplain Meesen put on a mask and went into the tunnels, gradually filling with yellow smoke as he hurried towards twelve. The lamp he carried proved almost useless. He kept his right hand touching the wall, feeling his way.

At the junction where the tunnel from twelve met the main tunnel Meesen bumped into Commandant Van der Auwera.

"Will you let me go to the wounded?" asked Meesen. Van der Auwera assented and said he would go along. They passed the steel hatch to the casemate. "There are no more Belgians here", Meesen said, listening intently.

"No, but there are Germans", Van der Auwera whispered.

They started to climb the stairs, Van der Auwera ahead of Meesen. Van der Auwera showed great courage, picking his way upward, stair by stair, looking cautiously about, unawed by the fact a machine gun burst from above or an explosion might kill him. It was a touchy situation.

They heard voices above. They inched upward, Meesen's hand touching Van der Auwera lightly so as not to run into him.

"Who's there; who's there? Van der Auwera called. Arendt stood at the head of the shaft with his companions. They jumped back against the wall. Belgians and Germans froze.

Van der Auwera crept along, his pistol pointed upward. Meesen grabbed the Commandant's belt to prevent him from rashly endangering himself.

"Never mind", Van der Auwera whispered, "they have placed a barrier above", and he flashed a light on the planking one story above. "You see, they can't come down".

They climbed three more steps. "Look out"! Meesen shouted as an object sped past into the depths. A deafening explosion raised the stairs underfoot. Each managed to hold on to the rail and kept from falling. Their search was finished. Helmetless, feeling with hands and feet, they finally made it to the bottom. It was pitch black. They stumbled over debris trying to put more distance between them and the shaft, expecting any moment to have a grenade explode. At last, Van der Auwera, out of breath, thoroughly shaken, puffed, "Come, we must rest here". They sat down. Meesen could hear Van der Auwera's labored breathing. After a while they got up and felt their way through the steel door barrier. Meesen helped Van der Auwera clear away the debris around the doors. With much effort they finally got both doors closed.

"They can throw their grenades now, I am almost deaf", said Van der Auwera, and the two turned upwards towards the Command Post.

Officers of Fort Eben Emael taken at the Fallingbostel prisoner of war camp in Germany. Top row—Debrez, Dehousse, Legaie, Michaux. Middle row—Polis, Deuse, De Sloovere, Ventsraeten, Mouton. Bottom row—Delcourt, Vamecg, Jottrand, Hotermans, Lavaque, Quitin.

11. COUNTER ATTACK!

Jottrand's information about the enemy was sketchy. Reports from the besieged Fort were fragmentary, or distorted. Even truthfully reported incidents rang false, so fantastic was the power, so unusual the nature of the German attack. A single mysterious charge exploded with such unheard of violence that it crippled massive emplacements built to withstand the pounding of the heaviest artillery then known, the piercing effect of the largest caliber antitank shells or the biggest air bombs.

The Belgians that day never did guess what it was the Germans had that could be so destructive. Based on reports flowing in from his sergeants and officers and from Belgian forces in the vicinity of the Fort who infrequently caught glimpses of the glidermen, it became evident to Jottrand that, though their power was incalculable, the Germans on the surface were few in number.

By 0800 Jottrand was able to establish some semblance of order, and began to grope for means to seize the initiative and, hopefully, retake the Fort. More information was essential. At about this time he got a call from Liège peremptorily ordering him to ". . . clean out the damned Germans" from the top of the Fort. Headquarters was under the impression that the German attack as well as the size of the attacking force had been grossly over-rated.

To get a better idea of the situation Jottrand dispatched Lieutenant Mouton to nineteen to make a reconnaissance. He got as far as the entrance to the stairwell to the casemate where he found no sign of the enemy, *but did not ascend to the gun chambers.* Mouton returned to Jottrand and gave a sketchy report. Jottrand, furious, dressed down the officer for having failed to make a more thorough reconnaissance.

He sent him back at 0900. (It was a 40 minute round trip to nineteen from Jottrand's location). Jottrand made it quite clear to the Lieutenant that he wanted a thorough reconnaissance and the Lieutenant must tell him if the guns were operable and if it was feasible to get men out from there to the surface of the Fort. This time Jottrand sent two sergeants along with the officer.

The three trudged to the casemate and cautiously crawled into the gun chamber. They saw frightful carnage in the rays of light that penetrated a huge hole blasted through the three-foot-thick concrete. The walls were scorched. Many inches of dust, concrete and scrap metal littered the floor. They heard nothing outside. Mouton crept up the slender steel ladder to the observation cupola. He heard gutteral German voices. He slipped back to the gun room, signalled his men to follow, and withdrew.

With Mouton's report and those from Meesen and Van der Auwera, Jottrand realized that the possibility of retaking any of the casemates seemed slim. Belgians trying to retake a position would have to climb 60 to 90 feet of stairs perhaps with Germans looking down their throats all the way. What Jottrand feared most was that the Germans might make an entry in force through one or several unmanned casemates and endanger or capture twenty-three and others that were operable. Such a sally could, if aggressively carried out by the Germans, force the Fort's surrender.

Jottrand moved to do what he could to protect the interior. He ordered the tunnels sealed with the steel barriers provided for this type of enemy attack. Along the tunnels between these barriers and his command post and other critical installations he ordered sandbag revetments to be built. In all he had 18 revetments built and manned.

Jottrand, as anxious as Liège to rid the Fort of its tormentors, had no infantrymen or even artillerymen trained in infantry tactics to go about the task of routing out the Germans. Unfortunately, he was the victim of a doctrinal decision of the Belgian Army.

After the first World War a great debate had raged in the Belgian Army on the subject of whether fortress commanders should have infantry units in their forts to take on just such a task as Jottrand now was ordered to do. After many years the army settled on the doctrine that infantry would not be assigned to the forts and that infantry missions, such as manning the outer defenses of a fort or making counter attacks to assist the artillerymen within the fort, should come from mobile divisions nearby. Thus, the men in the Fort had been well trained in the artillery and technical schools of Belgium to fire the guns and operate the Fort's intricate systems, but had no infantry training.

Jottrand, nevertheless, carried out his orders. He directed Lieutenant Verstraeten to make the counterattack. The lieutenant called for volunteers. Few responded. Two sergeants who did were asked to circulate and scare up some more men. Verstraeten finally mustered twelve. Armed only with carbines, they left the Fort and, hugging the wall, turned north towards casemate four. At 0900 one of the patrol waved his hand to Verstraeten and then pointed to the casemate. Moving to where he could get a better view Verstraeten saw a German, probably Sergeant Arendt, on top of the casemate so absorbed in his work he was oblivious to the presence of the Belgians. He took off before they could shoot. The explosion from the charge Arendt had placed was so violent the Belgians thought it must have been fired from an unusually large howitzer.

Since his patrol was lightly armed, and with Belgian artillery falling at his front and Stukas diving at him, the officer decided to fall back. Jottrand's anger flared when he realized how timorous the attack had been and how little information Verstraeten had brought. He ordered Verstraeten back to the surface. In the interval of a few minutes, however, Verstraeten's men had evaporated into the gloomy recesses of the Fort.

A new force had to be constituted. At 0930 Verstraeten and Sergeant L'Hereuse, as second in command, with a small force cautiously sallied out. He retraced his route. One of the Belgians saw troops to the west moving towards the entrance to the Fort. Verstraeten, fearing that an enemy force might cut off his line of withdrawal, instructed his men to turn back. At the entrance he met Captain Wagemans, commanding a force of 40 grenadiers. The Captain had been ordered to counter-attack the Germans on the Fort but, unacquainted with the area, especially the surface of the Fort, requested guides. Jottrand assigned Verstraeten and Lieutenant Deuse who now guided Wagemans to positions where they could launch an attack. At 1030 the force moved out.

Despite the fact he had no grenades, and only light weapons and was constantly harassed by Stukas, Wagemans took the force along the west wall of the Fort. When half way to position four he halted, divided his unit, giving part to Lieutenant Verstraeten, who then moved back towards position three. There, Verstraeten and his men crept on top of the Fort and got to the vicinity of positions twelve and nine and fired on suspected German positions. At 1015 Verstraeten got hit. He returned to the Fort.

Wagemans, meanwhile, in the woods along the west wall could hear some firing on the southwest surface of the Fort, probably from Verstraeten's men, but could not coordinate his attack with them. He surmised something had gone wrong with Verstraeten.

At 1300 Wagemans came upon Lieutenant Deuse who was attending a seriously wounded soldier. Deuse left and returned with two aid men and a stretcher.

For the remainder of the day the vigilant Stukas kept Wagemans from launching a single productive attack. Any aggressive move was immediately countered by a screaming Stuka. By nightfall his men were parched and exhausted. He ordered them to withdraw towards the entrance of the Fort. He sent one of his sergeants to find Jottrand and seek the Major's permission to enter the Fort. Jottrand was firm. He would only take the wounded. Wagemans' force might seriously overtax the Fort's facilities. Wagemans wearily made his way to his regiment.

Periodically through the day Jottrand called in artillery fire of the sister Forts Pontisse and Barchon at some miles distant from Fort Eben Emael. Some of the salvos called for were to keep Witzig's men under cover so as to keep them from becoming too aggressive. Needless to say, their requests for artillery support were totally unexpected to Pontisse and Barchon for neither had imagined they would ever be requested to fire directly on Fort Eben Emael so early in an attack.

The artillery fire had a sobering effect on Witzig who, with such a small force, could see his tenuous hold seriously endangered. Like any seasoned soldier, he also had a sneaking suspicion this artillery was no harassing fire, but was the prelude to an infantry attack. He shifted his forces accordingly.

Jottrand was eager to obtain better results and decided to place the responsibility of organizing a new force on Van der Auwera. He went from one area to another seeking volunteers.

Finally Lieutenant De Sloovere, Gigon, Legaie, several non-commissioned officers and 20 men, under Van der Auwera left the Fort. Forts Pontisse and Barchon had, by now, ceased firing. Although grenades were scarce, Van der Auwera managed to get a few, but his force had no machine guns.

Realizing that the interior of casemate twelve was held by the Germans, Van der Auwera, nevertheless, ordered a part of his force to its embankment and directed them to fire at the Germans in the north to attract their attention. Taking the rest of the men he moved back to three and there climbed on to the surface of the Fort to attack casemate nine. Leaving a non-commissioned officer and five men to protect his rear at the top of casemate six he maneuvered his force towards nine.

The whole operation lacked spirit and drive. Men responded to orders half-heartedly, took undue precautions, and made Van der Auwera's efforts a thankless job. Many refused to budge when ordered, lying terrified on the grass. Sergeant Hermesse at position twelve, was hit and withdrew to the Fort leaving De Sloovere there with only three men. The Lieutenant observed Germans moving in what appeared to be an effort to dislodge him. He and his men tossed their precious grenades. Van der Auwera dashed over to tell them to conserve their ammunition, but too late. They had already thrown all their grenades. Meanwhile, De Sloovere could hear a German shouting orders from the other side of the slope. He simultaneously heard one or more flare pistols pop and in seconds red flares burst overhead, smoky trails spiraling downward after them. This brought the Stukas. Van der Auwera looked about and quickly reassessed his situation. His initial force had dwindled to *himself, De Sloovere, Legaie, one non-commissioned officer and four enlisted men!* The others had vanished!

At about 1715 Van der Auwera reluctantly started withdrawing. His effort had not proved entirely unrewarding. De Sloovere captured a German machine gun, others had found some German explosives. Under cover of the Fort they had a chance to look at a photo taken from a dead German. To everyone's amazement, it was a picture of Fort Eben Emael with casemates and other defenses clearly visible.

Sorely pressed to get results that only a good-sized counter-attack could achieve Jottrand decided to order the men at Wonck to attack. At 1300 or thereabouts he called Wonck and ordered Levaque to hurry the badly needed reserve to the Fort. At 1345 Levaque marched at the head of 233 men. In one hour at a stepped-up cadence, they would be in the Fort. The distance was only three miles. The column carried two machine guns, three automatic rifles and each man had a carbine.

Stukas terrorized the column almost as soon as it started. The Belgians took the beating bravely but the march slowed to a crawl as men frequently fanned out into the fields to avoid the bombs. It was not until 1600 hours that Lieutenant Levaque and fifteen others reached the questionable "sanctuary" of the Fort's interior. Others dribbled in later. The number swelled to 100 by nightfall. The dishevelled appearance of the garrison from Wonck did not help the morale of the garrison for they realized that the situation was going equally badly for the Belgians outside.

Even as the mauled force from Wonck arrived at the gate, Lieutenant Levaque had a message thrust at him by Lieutenant Polis. "Get to the top of the Fort at once and clear out the enemy!" Levaque permitted his men to take a few minutes rest after their demoralizing trek. When Captain Hotermans went about reassembling them to make his attack on the surface, even with the aid of Lieutenants Levaque and Quitin, the task proved utterly discouraging. The soldiers took every evasive measure they could to avoid being detected and dragged into ranks again. The officers themselves, not convinced of the wisdom of the operation and also distraught and tired, nevertheless rounded up about 100 men.

At 1745, passing those from Van der Auwera's force now straggling in, by twos and threes Levaque's men ran from the tunnel to an assembly point near position three and maneuvered towards twelve. Off in the distance Levaque got a glimpse of Wagemans' grenadiers, but made no effort to coordinate his attack with them. Darkness was closing in. There was little time left and he doubted that coordination would accomplish anything worthwhile.

He decided to attack the enemy in casemate twelve. To his dismay, only eight men agreed to follow him. Their advance was soon stopped. The Germans sprayed them from all sides with machine gun fire. Pinned down, one by one, the Belgians withdrew to the slope just below twelve. The Stukas then began to take over. The force endured a terrifying hour of bombing after which the men, as well as they could, made their way into the Fort. Levaque made his report to Hotermans. It was 1845.

In a mood of desperation Captain Hotermans, with the aid of Lieutenants Levaque, Gigon and Quitin, accompanied by a few non-commissioned officers, circulated among the men trying to enlist volunteers. Surprisingly, 60 responded. They moved to the exit and waited but the Stukas returned, perhaps sensing the Belgians' intentions. Bomb after bomb exploded at the exit preventing anyone from leaving. Not deterred, Jottrand ordered Levaque to move his force through the tunnels towards casemate four. That casemate had an exit to the outside of the Fort. It had been put there by the designer for just such an emergency and would enable a Belgian counterattacking force to get out from the interior to the outside of the Fort at a place less likely to be under German observation. Levaque started his force through the tunnels. Half way there his force was blasted by a jet of air and a resounding explosion coming from the casemate towards which they were heading.

Apparently sensing the Belgians would make this attempt, Witzig had ordered Sergeant Harlos to set another charge against four. This was the blast that caught Levaque's force. Hotermans halted Levaque and, alone, went forward into the casemate. He found a gaping hole where the exit should have been. Realizing Germans were close at hand, he ordered a sand bag barrier built in the tunnel and manned it heavily with men from Levaque's force to prevent the Germans from getting inside the tunnel. He gave up further thought of counterattacking via this exit.

After an interlude of some hours, during which time he consolidated his position, Witzig turned his attention to the casemate seventeen which commanded the Canal. Sergeant Henrotay, and those who kept the 60-mm cannon and the machine guns in operation there, proved to be the last thorny tactical problem for the Germans to solve. It took the undivided attention of Witzig, and of the German forces along the ridge of the Canal's other bank who were also attempting to find some way of liquidating the position. Witzig realized that as long as seventeen remained in operation, the help from German ground forces was in jeopardy.

Witzig set Harlos to the task and a knotty one it proved to be. Harlos first lowered a hollow charge over the wall on a rope wound with prima cord connected to the fuse of the charge. He managed to get the charge alongside the projecting concrete and explode it but with absolutely no result. The gun continued to fire without perceptible let-up. Three times he tried this dangerous operation, endangered by Belgian fire from thirty-five, the companion casemate farther to the south along the Canal, and also from Belgian positions near Canne. The casemate continued to operate despite the German attacks.

Sporadically throughout the day the 75's in twenty-three would come to life shooting at Witzig's glidermen or firing volley's at German columns. This worried Witzig and upon Niedermeier's suggestion Witzig gave him permission to take another try at destroying the guns.

With List, Graef, and Stucke, the Sergeant crept through the brush along a small hollow leading to the casemate. He halted nearby and watched. The dome rose to fire every two minutes. He and his men crept nearer to place a charge for the *coup de grace* when the cupola was down, when all of a sudden a flight of Stukas, plane by plane, started unleashing 500-pound bombs at the dome.

The Germans fled. After the Stuka attack Niedermeier returned, "anxious to tangle with the rascal". But now "hell broke loose from other quarters". An enemy machine gun somewhere outside the Fort was "beginning to sound its blessing". Unable to advance he and his men gave up the effort and returned to their casemate.

At 1300 casemate four came to life. Apparently the Belgians had repaired the damage from Arendt's attack. Witzig sent Gramse from Harlos' Squad to see if he could silence four. Gramse moved through the woods and put a 25-pound hollow charge against one of the embrasures. It silenced the work for three hours.

Jottrand requested and soon got a heavy concentration of artillery fire from Forts Pontisse and Barchon to soften German resistance just prior to Levaque's attack.

Around 2015 Major Jottrand issued orders for the night. He established a guard system to assure constant and vigilant manning of the barricades. He arranged for regular relief of crews at gun and observation sites, directing that he be immediately informed of German activity. To keep the enemy from becoming too bold, he saw to it that remaining operable guns of his shattered forces fired periodically. He got interdiction fire from Fort Pontisse to discourage Witzig from becoming too enterprising during the night.

From inside the Fort men could hear machine gun fire and shells exploding sporadically, primarily from the direction of the Canal. There was no certainty whether the fire was from German weapons pounding away at seventeen, or from its defenders.

Thirty-three was frequently illuminated by brilliant flares, some set off by the Belgians, others by the Germans. Occasionally rounds from German artillery fell close.

Despite all the defensive measures taken by the Belgians that should have immobilized a force ten times superior to Witzig's the Belgians grew more and more uneasy as the night wore on.

The hollow charge was an unknown weapon to the Belgians. Because they did not know what this horrible new weapon was, or where it would next take its toll the Belgians could never feel confident they could cope with their enemy. When the garrison began to relax a detail began to shuttle explosives towards eighteen, probably in order to place them in a more convenient location should they be needed, but the action served to send rumors flying that the Germans had started to enter the tunnels and that the tunnel leading to eighteen was to be blown. This heightened the tension.

When, at 0200, a terrifying explosion shook the Command Post and all the installations of the Fort in the vicinity of the entrance, imagination ran rampant. It had apparently come from German artillery behind the walls at the mill. The machine guns and 60's of twenty-two immediately returned fire and guns in the entrance casemate and at six opened up to discourage an enemy infantry assault from the direction of nineteen from reaching the Fort's walls. Major Jottrand, as a precautionary measure, now expecting a heightened German activity, sent officers around to each barricade. His orders were to "Resist at all costs!"

Shortly thereafter new rumblings could be heard coming from the recesses of the Fort. Rumors spread wildly. "Germans had crossed the Canal and with some demonic means had begun to tunnel under the Fort! "Everybody would be blown sky high." No less than Chief Surgeon, Dr. Steegen who should have been the most rational of the besieged garrison, imagined this to be true.

12. THE GLIDERMEN TAKE CONTROL

Casemate twenty-six, housing three 75-mm howitzers, almost got by unmolested by the Germans. There is a strong possibility it might not have suffered its fate as early as the other Belgian installations except for Wenzel's alertness when he found that Sergeant Maier's Squad had not reached the Fort. It was Maier's Squad that was to attack twenty-six. Witzig's plan provided for this unforeseen development. He had given Unger's team the additional mission of attacking twenty-six should Maier's outfit not be able to do so. But, as noted above, Unger was dead and Else was in serious trouble and unable to attack twenty-six.

A combination of Belgian misjudgment and indecision within twenty-six offset the temporary German setback. Belgian inaction lasted long enough for the overworked men of Squad Ten to engage the casemate. Although 21 Belgians of the howitzer crews had their crews ready to fire at 0435, nevertheless explosions they took to be from diving Stuka bombs drove them to the level below the guns. The explosions undoubtedly came from the charges exploding against other Belgian cupolas and casemates.

Lieutenant De Sloovere, who had come from the Headquarters of the Fort, ordered that all the guns be manned. De Sloovere, with the aid of Sergeant Delcourt, fired two 75's. The third was unserviceable. De Sloovere received a call to return to

Headquarters, and firing ceased. The idle men became nervous. Their crew chief sent them to the safer intermediate level.

Sensing a change of pace in twenty-six's operations, Heuble used the lapse in Belgian action to rush it. Reaching the casemate, he and several men inserted two pound charges into each gun tube. The explosion disabled the howitzers and created choking fumes.

At 0510 Jottrand gave firing orders to the Fort's artillery. Since no one in twenty-six was at gun stations he heard no sound from the 75's. This caused Jottrand to conclude that twenty-six had been blown and at 0540 he reported to Headquarters at Liège that it was destroyed and abandoned.

However, unbeknownst to Jottrand, the crew remained in the second level, still close to their guns. About 1000 Lieutenant Legaie arrived from the Command Post, ordered by Major Van der Auwera to survey the situation. The crew chief reported that Germans occupied the gun room and he had sealed off the casemate from below. Legaie ran back to Van der Auwera and described the situation. Van der Auwera ordered De Sloovere to retake twenty-six. De Sloovere ordered his crew chief to ready his men for the venture. The Sergeant, stupefied, muttered, "But the enemy is in the casemate!" De Sloovere, ignoring the non-com's response, and accompanied by two volunteers, set out on the dangerous task of pulling down the barriers. The three, probing cautiously ahead ascended the stairwell peering for the enemy, carbines at the ready. They arrived at the gun chamber and to their surprise, found absolutely no one. Listening intently, however, De Sloovere heard gutteral German voices outside. He was uncertain if his presence had been discovered but he did not budge. The two soldiers had lagged behind and now De Sloovere was quite alone.

He searched for shells and found a dozen. He took one, put it into the firing device and set it for a muzzle burst. He went

German engineers attempt a crossing of the Albert Canal under fire from casemate 17.

to the center gun, stealthily opened and pulled back the breech, slid the round in the chamber, quickly slammed the breech and pulled the lanyard. One by one, as fast as he could go, he continued firing until the supply was exhausted. He then listened but could not detect the presence of any Germans. At 1030 De Sloovere got orders from Jottrand to return to headquarters to be ready to participate in counterattacks.

The Germans never bothered about nine and its twin, twenty-nine since they were limited to firing to the south and offered no threat to the bridges.

Twenty-three kept busy. Observers along the Belgian lines, noting a pontoon bridge beginning to reach across the Meuse at the Belgian side, called for artillery and the cupola began harassing the German bridging unit. In the same way it began pounding away at German units making their way through Holland just across the Meuse. It silenced one German machine gun 400 yards southwest that had been firing at remote casemate thirty-two and the southern part of the Fort. So exhausting was the job of keeping the two 75's operating at such a pace, so debilitating the smoke-filled gun room, that Sergeants Fourir and Hanot and new gun crews relieved the regular crew at 1100. That night Sergeant Joiris and another relief replaced the second crew. Lieutenant Delrez, after an inspection trip to the cupola, reported that so much ammunition had been fired that there were no more shrapnel shells and other ammunition was running low. Its greatest contribution was the deadly fire it had placed on the German held positions on top of the Fort itself.

Periodically, the crews lowered the 75's and swept the surface firing on positions eighteen, twenty-six, thirty and cupola twenty-four. This was the best argument the Belgians had to convince Witzig not to become too aggressive. Witzig, as we have seen, heeded the warning but that did not negate the hard fact that the most important tactical guns of the Fort which could pound the bridges and targets to the north, had been effectively silenced and were unable to get back into action. Fire from remote casemate thirty-three continued to harass, disrupt and slow down the German onslaught. German intelligence finally singled it out. Stukas took it on, bomb after bomb falling on and around the lone outpost, the blanket of dust and smoke they raised billowing high above the concrete, blinding the observers and serving, in a way, to meet the German objective of destroying this position's effectiveness. The bombs never did drive its observers from this hotly attacked site and it kept operating to the end.

Although the Germans failed to prevent the Belgians from destroying the bridge at Canne because of Jottrand's dogged determination to see it destroyed, they succeeded brilliantly in taking the two other bridges intact. Captain Koch landed at Vroenhoven with four other officers and 129 men. This force included Lieutenant Schacht's platoon, whose mission was to take the bridge. While Koch and several of the force went about establishing the command post and gaining radio contact with the three other glider forces, Lieutenant Schacht, went about the capture of the bridge. The operations had been prepared with such unbelievable detail and the Belgians were so overwhelmed that the Germans disarmed the explosives on the bridge in a few minutes after the landings. Less than 30 minutes later the bridge was open to German tanks and within three hours all significant Belgian resistance in the area was liquidated. Despite strong Belgian efforts to dislodge the glidermen, the Germans held firm. However, the Schacht unit paid a heavy price losing seven killed and 18 wounded.

Sergeant Pirenne set off the charges inserted into the bridge at Canne just as the gliders were landing. It was touch and go as to whether he would succeed. The Germans encountered some minor delay getting out of their gliders and into the attack on the bridge and because of this the bridge was blown.

A short time after he landed, Koch's radio operator had the reassuring signal from Wenzel at Fort Eben Emael. Thenceforth word was received intermittently that Witzig's force was maintaining control. However, Koch had no word from Lieutenant Schacht at the Canne bridge. About noon Koch sent a patrol to establish contact with Schacht to find out what had occurred there. Two hours passed. The patrol returned. Its commander reported the bridge was demolished, and Schacht's team had taken a beating. The patrol found four glidermen dead and located six others severely wounded. Schacht's glidermen were disappointed at not having captured the bridge. Nevertheless before they were relieved on the 11th, they had captured 49 officers and 250 men and left 150 Belgians killed.

At Veldwezelt German success was comparable to that at Vroenhoven. Several Belgian officers, hearing the alert signaled by the Fort's guns, were prompted to press for permission to blow the bridge immediately. They were dissuaded by a senior officer who advised them that it was necessary to get a formal order first. The order never came, and the gliders were overhead and into the midst of the surprised defenders before they could take action on their own. The glider assemblage above them virtually hypnotized the gawking Belgians into inaction None could venture a guess as to what the mysterious silent birds were, for none had ever seen airplanes without engines.

Lieutenant Altmann's glidermen landed according to plan Using the hollow charge against the casemate protecting the bridge, and aggressively attacking the entrenched Belgians, Altmann captured the bridge in ten minutes. The Belgian Army suffered heavy casualties and many civilians in the surrounding area were killed or wounded while the bridge was under attack. In the combat that ensued during the remainder of the day the Germans suffered eight dead and 21 wounded.

The action of the German Luftwaffe at Lanaeken was largely responsible for the failure of the Belgians to destroy the bridges. Commandant Giddeloo who was charged with the bridges at Veldwezelt and Vroenhoven, had his headquarters at Lanaeken. His location was apparently well-known to the Luftwaffe through German intelligence. Gideloo was promptly informed by one of his observers in an outpost along the Canal that the Germans were landing near one of the bridges. Just as the word reached him, four Stukas, one by one, peeled off from formation high above Lanaeken and one after the other dove unerringly at Giddeloo's headquarters releasing their bombs. Their aim was perfect, undoubtedly sharpened by months of practice for just this one mission, and the headquarters disintegrated under the force of the explosions. Giddeloo and 20 Belgians were blown apart just as he began to transmit orders to the guards at the bridges. Some months earlier, during the course of an inspection, Giddeloo had complained that his headquarters was virtually unprotected from an attack.

"Are you afraid, Giddeloo?" his superior officer asked.

"No, but I can tell you", Giddeloo pounded the table, "that the war will start by surprise, and I am certain it will begin here!" He was right.

13. "P" MEIER'S PRIVATE WAR

It was about 1100 when a somewhat garbled message came through to Lieutenant Witzig. The message, hardly more than a rumor, placed Corporal "P" Meier, a member of missing Squad Two, somewhere near the west wall of the Fort. It was not until several days later that the story of Squad Two could be pieced together. Squad Two's glider had been cast off prematurely and pilot Bredenbeck had used his remaining speed and altitude to get the best landing he could. The glider landed in a field between Düren and the hamlet of Soller. A German driving a motorcycle with sidecar stopped and gazed in wonder at the Martian-like crew and craft. Before the bewildered man knew what was happening he found himself with two passengers, Sergeant Max Maier and Corporal "P" Meier, as the latter was dubbed to distinguish him from his Squad leader. Off they sped to Düren and to the German police commissioner's office. Their sudden appearance, in uniform so unlike any German uniform he had ever seen, their request for a fast car, took the officer at the desk aback. "He didn't feel he had the authority—after all, theirs was a military task . . . !" He went on, making it clear to Sergeant Max Maier he was wasting time. Several telephone calls failed to reach a suitable military headquarters. They jumped on the motorcycle and took off to a military caserne the cyclist knew. There, they were again frustrated by obtuseness and red tape for which German officialdom was famous. Embittered, they sped to another caserne. This one belonged to German Army Engineers. There a lieutenant managed to find two civilian cars for them. Returning to the remainder of the Squad, the Sergeant loaded them in the two vehicles and the road-bound glider unit sped through Düren and towards Belgium. Outside Düren they were slowed down by columns of advancing German tanks, trucks and marching men. In and out they wove until they were leading the column. Near Maastricht they abandoned the cars, got to the Meuse on foot, and persuaded the engineer assault unit to put them in the first boats the Germans sent across. Once on the other side they teamed up with the infantry to clear out the Belgians.

In the market place they found a Dutch truck driver whom they forced to drive them toward the Fort. Near Canne they began to encounter some enemy firing but pressed on into the town. As they moved toward the bridge the Squad encountered a Belgian soldier who had no will to fight. He was interrogated and told them more of his companions were under cover close by. When assured none would be mistreated he whistled several times and 40 armed Belgians timidly straggled in from many directions and were made prisoners.

The Squad proceeded cautiously towards the bridge at Canne to find it folded into the river. Nothing daunted Max Maier ordered the rest of the Squad into a defensive position, told them to cover him, and he gingerly started to pick his way along the bridge girders to get to the other side. The Belgians spotted him and he quickly got their undivided attention. He went only a few yards before he was hit twice. He painfully made his way back, falling on the gravel shore close to the pilings. Private Gehlich, braving the fire, crouched low and dashed to Maier's side. The Sergeant waved him away, his strength ebbing rapidly. "It's too late—take cover. Just leave me here". A few minutes later "P" Meier started across the bridge by himself. He touched Max's hand affectionately as he passed. There was no response now. Max was dead.

Getting across the bridge, and stealing a bicycle in Canne, Meier pedaled into the village of Eben Emael racing between columns of marching Belgian soldiers who were bewildered by his appearance. Dumbfounded at this unexpected visitor in their ranks, perhaps not certain that the singular uniform might be an old Belgian one, or whatever the reason, none chose to challenge Meier. Stukas shrieked and he, with the Belgians, dove for cover. Meier found himself flat on his face, at arms length from his enemies. The attack over, he mounted his bicycle again and pedaled on, trying to find his way to the Fort.

He soon found the road to the Fort and becoming more cautious, dismounted and walked to the heavily damaged barracks.

He did not see any German glidermen. He searched the area for a few minutes, realizing he might be discovered at any moment. He pulled the orders of 10 May, 1940 for the garrison of Eben Emael from a bulletin board as evidence he had been there, and made his way cautiously on foot back to the bridge. He dove through the door of a damaged house to get protection from a Stuka. The explosion blew down one of the walls and threw a beam across his leg. Fortunately he was able to free himself. His leg was not broken but was severely injured. He limped towards the bridge. As he approached it he began to scan the opposite shore for his comrades. He could see none of them. All were deeply dug in to take protection from the heavy Belgian fire. Meier got behind a wall from where he tried to discover the whereabouts of the squad. A large shell hit the wall and knocked him flat on his back showering him with rubble.

Unable to raise his Squad he trudged back towards the Fort

The bridge at Canne after its destruction by the Belgians on May 10, 1940.

along the Canal towpath. He left the path and went south into the swampy area betwen the Geer River and the Fort, and then east to the Fort. Sergeant Wenzel spotted Meier but did not recognize him in the brush. He ordered his light-machine gunner beside him to take aim. Now, Meier rose above the brush and hailed Wenzel. Wenzel was about to give the order to fire but, on second thought, he placed his hand on the gunner's arm, saying, "Don't shoot. I don't want to kill such a brave man", unaware that he had almost ordered his comrade's execution. Realizing that it would be useless to advance any further Meier, undismayed, turned south where he finally found Sergeant Haug in the woods close to Casemate four. However, the moat lay between him and the Fort, preventing Meier from getting to Haug. Nevertheless, Meier gave Haug the story of his misfortunes and assured him that he and the others would join Granite when the Canal was crossed.

Meier turned again towards the bridge. Looking across the Canal he saw German ground units apparently stalled by the water. He motioned and yelled to them to cross. For all his effort he drew a hail of fire which he was able to avoid by diving into a ditch nearby. He cautiously rose again and beckoned. This time the Germans held their fire. They had finally recognized him as a fellow German. He shouted to them to cross. They answered, "It's too dangerous".

Furious at their timidity, he sidled back along the bridge girders hoping to find his Squad and lead them to the Fort. However, the Belgians had renewed their attacks against the Germans in this area and Meier, got pinned down and was unable to recross the Canal. From that time on he was not certain of the whereabouts of the rest of his Squad, although he thought they were still close at hand. Each time he raised his head he would draw a fusilade of shots from the Belgians.

Meanwhile, during Meier's absence, his Squad kept themselves profitably occupied. They moved their 40 prisoners to the northwest edge of Canne.

In the early afternoon the first elements of German engineers began to appear in Canne and the vicinity of the blown bridge. At first they were unaware of the presence of Meier's Squad and were soon firing on Schacht's glidermen on the other bank mistaking them for Belgians. Corporal Bader, in charge during Meier's absence, shouted German oaths so loudly that he finally gained their attention. He got to their commander who, finally convinced that the "enemy" on the other side really were Germans, ordered his men to stop firing. Although none of his Squad was hit, several Belgians were. When some German engineers arrived, they agreed to take the prisoners off Bader's hands. Bader now took refuge under the girders of the destroyed bridge. At about midnight Belgian artillery made three "bullseyes" on the girders right above him and he was injured. He crawled out when the fire let up and made his way back towards Canne where he met some German engineers who told him that they had seen some paratroopers going to the main aid station in Maastricht. He proceeded to Maastricht and at the aid station was bandaged, and then returned to Canne, unable to find the rest of his buddies in the village. About 200 yards from the bridge he leaped through the doorway of a shattered cottage to escape artillery fire and found himself in the midst of eight Belgians. They surrendered at his command.

"Are there any more around?" Bader asked.

"Yes", one of them answered.

"Tell them the village is surrounded and their resistance is useless", Bader said. With this the Belgian called loudly from the doorway several times and 100 Belgians, with their arms raised, started trickling in from all directions. Bader assured the terrified Belgians that they would not be shot.

He ordered them to fall in and went down the ranks disarming the men, any one of them could have killed him immediately. He turned them towards Maastricht and marched them off. He got to the city where he encountered the Major of a construction battalion and asked the officer what to do with the prisoners. He was told to go to the prisoner collection point and was given direction. He got there to find only a medical company. He was referred to a prisoner-of-war camp in Bergen. Somehow he got the help of two other men and reached Bergen with a total of 121 prisoners, a few others having been gathered enroute. There he found a prisoner-of-war collection point. He turned his men over to the commander but not before he got a receipt for them afraid that unless he had this evidence no one would ever believe his story. He attached this receipt to his combat report which he gave to Lieutenant Witzig some days later.

14. THE BLITZKRIEG CATCHES UP

Except for Haug's brief encounter with P. Meier earlier in the day, and some reassuring radio messages, Lieutenant Witzig had little evidence that help would come in time. True, he had discouraged the Belgian counterattack to this point, but there was a question as to how long he could hold out. The drinking water was exhausted, and he did not have sufficient ammunition left for any prolonged defense.

Colonel Melzer, Commander of the 151st Infantry Regiment of the 4th Armored Division, with the 51st Engineer Battalion attached under the command of Lieutenant Colonel Mikosch, had orders to get to Witzig. Stiff Belgian resistance and the destroyed bridges at Maastricht and at Canne slowed the German drive. However, two prongs of Mikosch's 51st Battalion were doing their best. By late afternoon of the 10th the Battalion had managed to get to Canne where a platoon under Sergeant Portsteffen broke off and moved south. His task was to cross the Canal somewhere near the northern point of the Fort and attempt to join up with the glidermen. The remainder of the Battalion was to cross at Canne, swing south and envelop the Fort from the southwest.

Sergeant Portsteffen made several attempts to launch inflated rubber assault craft across the Canal, but the Belgians all along the Canal, and especially at casemate seventeen, poured such withering fire on his men that he gave up. The embankment of the Canal over which the assault craft had to be lowered exposed his men for too long and made the project too hazardous.

At 1900 Lieutenant Moreau, a Belgian staff officer for the headquarters of the 7th Division inspected the position. His division commander was extremely worried about the new turn of events. The glider forces that were to take the bridge at Canne, had managed to cross there despite the fact that the Belgians had blown the bridge, and by 1600 had overrun the Belgian defenders under Lieutenant Gericot. There was now little protection for the Fort from the northwest. Moreau made it clear to Jottrand that the northwest wall of the Fort lay open to an impending German attack, and the defenders at casemate three should be especially vigilant. Since casemate four had been silenced the Fort was defenseless to the west and southwest.

As the Belgian fire intensified, many rounds hit the sides of the Canal, ricocheting crazily. At 2100 Portsteffen made another attempt to launch his boats but failed since the Belgians illuminated the area while seventeen poured fire on every suspicious movement.

About an hour late, when darkness had fallen and the Belgians were no longer able to see Portsteffen's platoon at work, his men moved their boats, now badly scarred, to a point above and across from the northern tip of the Fort.

A sharp whistle sent the engineers darting from their cover with their boats into which they tumbled hastily. Casting off, they started to paddle but they were soon spotted. Only a few hundred meters away, ahead and to their left, flashes appeared from the Fort. The thunder of firing soon resounded everywhere, dense smoke clouded the Canal bank behind them, and geysers of water burst upward as the artillery shells hit the water. They finally reached the opposite embankment. After reassembling, the attack troop worked its way unnoticed along the narrow edge of the bank bordering the northwest side of the Fort in order to skirt the flooded area around the Geer River. Finally, late that night, they arrived at the moat along the northwest wall. It was the last obstacle separating them from the dark and the foreboding Fortress ahead.

By morning, the men were joined by several glidermen. They were to try and silence casemate four to keep it from preventing a German attack on the Fort from the west.

In the tunnels below the casemate, as elsewhere throughout the Fort, the garrison's morale sagged successively lower under the sounds reaching them of the incessant pounding administered to the Fort. Soon, the increasing smoke seeping through the steel door of casemate four, became so unbearable that Sergeant Zone, in command of the Belgian detachment manning the sand-bagged guns sighted down the tunnel towards the doors of four, reported that the barricade had been blown. Although his report was erroneous, it served to heighten the concern at the Command Post that the Germans were now getting control of the interior.

Portsteffen's men, of the German ground forces, dropped explosives into casemate thirteen. This not only destroyed the stairs, but blew the doors and steel barriers off their supports. Crews from this and other installations to the north now began to withdraw towards the Fort's command post, leaving the Fort in the direction of the Canal defenseless. No barriers remained in some of the vital passageways between the Germans and the Belgians. The Germans, surmising that the Belgian resistance was crumbling, now resorted to terror tactics. They made entries where they could, firing small arms down the long dark tunnels, dropping heavy charges into entryways of emplacements into which they could not descend and, in every manner possible, kept up incessant noise and pressure to demoralize the defenders.

At 0800 the Chaplain made a round through the tunnels. The only light, came from his lamp. He could barely discern objects about because of the smoke. Close to the sealed doors in the tunnel below eighteen a small light hung. He heard voices and activity on the other side of the doors, apparently coming from Germans tearing away at the barrier set up there. Meesen turned back to the Command Post. Jottrand was burning secret military papers. Meesen now realized how serious the situation had become. Jottrand sent Meesen to check on the men at the 120's. He found them alert but frustrated, unable to use the guns. Whenever they tried to open the breeches to fire they could not be certain that a German grenade would not tumble out. This happened on several occasions and was a convincing deterrent to agressiveness.

Later, as Meesen stood near to Jottrand, a violent explosion shook everything. Lethal chunks of concrete rained all about. A wounded man passed them. Men challenged one another in the dark tunnels, uncertain if the sound ahead was friend or foe. No one seemed to have any idea of the actual situation. Lieutenant Quitin, carbine in hand, passed like a phantom and disappeared into the blackness. Anguish and fear were developing into stark terror. At 0800, Van der Auwera, Levaque and defenders of the sandbag barrier at twelve saw dense smoke coming from under the steel doors ahead.

On top of the Fort, Witzig and Portsteffen coordinated their plans for the remainder of the attack on the Fort. They went together from position to position relieving exhausted glidermen from those casemates in which they had been all through the night.

Arendt, knowing that help was soon to appear, exploded a 100-pound charge in the stairwell at casemate twelve. It blew

Two views of casemate 3, the entrance to Fort Eben Emael.

the shafts, ammunition elevator and the stairs into a tangle of wreckage. The charge was his parting gesture, and an action he had been aching to take since the day before. The force of the explosion blew out the steel doors and blew the officers and men at the sandbag barricade back into the interior of the Fort.

Captain Hotermans likened the effect of the explosion of a hollow charge at an extremity of a tunnel to that of the explosion of a bullet's propellant in a gun barrel. The expanding pressures from the explosion confined within the tunnel knocked some men flat, drove others ahead until the pressure subsided or the men hit a wall or other fixed obstacle, and caught up small debris driving it bullet fast down the tunnel.

A short time later Lieutenants Polis and Legaie, posted at eighteen, disheveled, staring vacantly, straggled in to tell Jottrand that the barriers there had been breached. De Sloovere came right behind to report an explosion at casemate twelve. The barrier defenders were strewn about. Sergeant Corombelle and Privates Dejardin, Massotte and Gillet were dead, the others unconscious. Close at hand Major Van der Auwera and Lieutenant Levaque, who had been on the way to check the situation at the casemate, lay shaken, Levaque burned, Van der Auwera had a concussion. Levaque painfully got on his feet. Van der Auwera, vacuously stammering firing orders at imaginery soldiers, was evidently out of his mind.

Barrels of chloride of lime, which was used to keep the interior sanitary, were broken in the explosions. Chlorine fumes began to seep into the already acrid, smoke-filled atmosphere. Men became drowsy, some developed painful, migraine-like headaches and found it increasingly difficult to keep alert at their posts. The tunnels were cluttered with debris. Men sat or stood waiting, some with wounds, making operations more and more difficult. Some of the men began to drift towards the Command Post while others remained at their posts, bravely holding on or unable to leave because their retreat was blocked.

Mikosch's force had turned south from Maastricht, reaching the vicinity of the blown bridge at Canne towards dusk. There, under light fire from the Belgian 2nd Grenadiers, he managed to force a crossing, using rubber assault boats. He disassembled much of his heavier equipment to shuttle it piecemeal over the Canal. By midnight, he had assembled his forces on the other bank. Melzer toiled energetically throughout the night. He positioned men and antitank guns under the support of artillery at Canne. He placed his high velocity antitank cannons behind the walls at the mill of Loverix, several hundred yards from the entrance to the Fort, to engage casemates three and six at dawn. In three, the entrance's defensive casemate, and the key to the defense of the whole southwest corner of the Fort, Sergeants Debarsy and Lecron stood heroically at their positions. The German anti-tank guns at Loverix, and a machine gun located in the ruins of Sergeant Lecron's shattered cottage subjected the casemate to a relentless pounding. Despite the danger, men stayed with their guns, firing on Portsteffen's unit who were making their way onto the surface of the Fort in the area around casemate four. Even after the Germans had taken the casemate, Degrange and Lecron continued to blast it, making the Germans pay a high price for having captured it.

At about 0800 Hotermans and De Sloovere arrived in the casemate. They took sightings out of the embrasures. They were there to find out at first hand what they could of the Germans. Why? Jottrand was setting up another attempt to launch a counterattack. Volunteers were again being rounded up in the Fort. However, after a brief survey and while these officers were in the casemate, a German anti-tank round tore into the casemate wall. Next, some grenades tumbled down past the main entrance.

Portsteffen's Germans had reached the entrance superstructure. When this was reported to Jottrand, he canceled his plan to counterattack.

While action was hot at the west walls the German antitank guns began a duel with the Belgians in Casemate thirty adjacent to the southeast wall. Sturdily constructed, virtually undamaged, and under the command of Sergeant Degrange, a strong-willed, dedicated soldier commanding a determined crew, casemate thirty demonstrated Belgian mettle. It sparred with machine and antitank guns located at several different points outside the Fort. One high velocity shell hit the west 60-mm cannon and knocked it out. It did not damage the machine gun in an embrasure just below, which kept up a devastating fire.

Later, a German shell penetrated the four-foot-thick reinforced concrete wall at some undetermined point, cut electric cables, plunged the casemate interior into darkness and stopped the ventilation system. Sergeant Degrange ordered his men to don masks, and back they went to the remaining guns. Before long, a shell exploded in the blackness, wounding Private Smets. Another hit the east embrasure and wedged between the 60-mm gun and the opening through which it protruded making it inoperable. German bullets kept pelting the embrasures throwing concrete chips and debris into the faces of the defenders. Ammunition was getting precariously low and, finally, the last machine gun quit operating. At 0930 Jottrand ordered thirty to be cleared and the tunnel leading to it barricaded. Thus a position critical to the continued and effective defense of the southeast wall of the Fort was silenced. Germans might be penetrating the tunnels from these casemates. The casemates around the Fort's walls were in heavy trouble. The situation was grim and deteriorating rapidly.

Twelve and eighteen had been reported destroyed. Jottrand displaying praiseworthy leadership, refused to be swayed by what might be inaccurate reports, the result of momentary hysteria, decided to see for himself. He courageously made his way into the danger-filled tunnels to twelve and eighteen. He found the situation not as bad as many reports had led him to believe. Only twelve had been totally destroyed and he saw no Germans. But if Germans were in the tunnels he realized they would then be able to fire right into the Command Post. Because of this, Jottrand went to the next lower level and established his headquarters. He directed several others of his staff to remain in the main command post to coordinate whatever remained of the Fort's artillery.

The Germans had not yet tested the Belgian's defenses within the interior of the fort near the command post. Lieutenants Quitin, Michaux and Debrez stayed at the fire direction center and others, such as Lieutenants Dehousse and Deuse remained at the barricades. Jottrand checked the men in the infirmary, and made rounds elsewhere so he could to keep his finger on the pulse of the garrison.

At 1020 an explosion destroyed the lower part of seventeen. Two men at the barricade below got seriously burned and the machine guns were torn apart. Lighting still was by flash light or an occasional hurricane lamp. An auxiliary ventilator that the maintenance crews had been able to start conked out, and efforts were made to get the main system in operation. It sputtered sporadically, but was ineffective in reducing the intense smoke. As the morning wore on the air became dense with the combination of smoke and chlorine. Men at the barricades coughing heavily, wheezing asthmatically, pleaded to be released to get into an area of the fort where they could breathe more freely. Their pleas fell on deaf ears. They were forced to stay and advised to wear their masks.

Pleas for reinforcements came from the defenders at the barriers. Twenty-five men were rounded up, but faded away, deserting into connecting passageways or niches here and there. One officer had disappeared. He was found under a bed. One sergeant got to his destination with three of the ten men who started with him.

By mid-morning the situation in the bowels of the Fort was desperate. A few heroic defenders still manned some barricades. Over-crowded, wounded and asphyxiated men were strewn on the floors of tunnels near the hospital. Passersby tripped over outthrust limbs, causing the wounded to moan in the darkness. Jottrand had called earlier for evacuation ambulances to help relieve the situation. The gesture was futile. None ever arrived. For Jottrand, the situation had deteriorated irretrievably. He stood alone and helpless. He drew consolation from those of his men who shouldered their tasks in a soldierly manner, but they were few, and their efforts, though sincere, could not alter the situation. Many men of the garrison, though able-bodied, were useless, either from combat fatigue, fear or lost hope.

Witzig's men had departed. German ground troops now were virtually ranging at will over the vast uncontested surfaces of the Fort, and in areas outside the walls.

At 0945 Jottrand reached his superior at Liège and demanded help—a counterattack—Fort Eben Emael needed relief! Survival, under the present circumstances, was now only a matter of time. Jottrand received a message at 1000 that indicated no help would be forthcoming. Whatever the truth of the matter, it is reported that Jottrand created the impression at Liège that the enemy had reached the Command Post of the Fort: "The Commandant had removed his Headquarters to the lower levels." In more urgent communications with Liège, Jottrand clearly outlined the conditions of the Fort in detail—he told them that prolongation of resistance was only building up Belgian casualties, with no commensurate gain, and with the enemy having nothing to lose. He mentioned that although some weapons, especially the 75's at casemate nine, were still operable

The shrine in honor of the Belgian defenders near the entrance to Fort Eben Emael.

as were the artillery direction center and some other facilities in the Fort, all else was inoperative. "The situation is desperate! In addition to 25 killed, there are four officers and 59 men wounded."

Again Jottrand pleaded, this time with the Commanding General. Although General De Krahe, the Belgian Commander of the III Army Corps, and his artillery commander, General Jadot, who coordinated the use of the Fort's artillery, were plagued with many equally stark problems, they directed their attention to the plight of the men now virtually entombed in the Fort. They reached the Commanding General of I Army Corps who was in direct command of the Fort. In a three party telephone hook-up they discussed the situation. There apparently was a great deal of equivocation. No one would assume responsibility for recommending the surrender of Fort Eben Emael. The implications were too enormous. The Commanding General of I Army Corps suggested they "take all necessary measures, with the concurrence of General De Krahe." Certainly a meaningless phrase—

Now General De Krahe, in a critical spot and not wanting to take the responsibility, stated the Fort was not under his direct command and that a decision to allow a capitulation depended on the General Headquarters of the Army. This solved nothing for Major Jottrand. General De Krahe ordered Captain Gheysen, one of his staff officers, to telephone General Headquarters, apprise them of the situation and get their decision. The Captain could not get anyone on the telephone, perhaps because General Headquarters itself knew the foreboding problem was looming and refused to be drawn into it to become thenceforth tainted. There the matter stood.

Taking matters into his own hands, as many a junior officer has had to do in a tight spot when higher command walks the tightrope of irresponsibility, Captain Gheyson drafted the following instruction: "Alone, only the Commander of the Fort can decide if it should cease its defense. He must consult his defense council. If there is a surrender the Commander of the Fort must blow up the works after it has been evacuated by its defenders."

While he had been writing the message a brief report arrived stating that German tank units were closing in on the Fort. Gheyson now added to the draft message the sombre sentence, "If the evacuation of the garrison is impossible, you are ordered to blow up the Fort and all its men."

Captain Gheyson showed the message to General De Krahe. The General approved and Captain Gheyson sent it to Jottrand.

Jottrand immediately summoned a council of defense in accordance with regulations established for emergencies at the Fort. Although all were fully aware of the content of articles pertaining to surrender, nevertheless Jottrand went through the formality of reading their provisions to those in attendance. What they might be about to do had deep implications to the welfare of the Belgian people. All stood by listening soberly, tears pouring from the eyes of some. Present were Doctor Willems, the head surgeon, Captain Vamecq, who took the place of Major Van der Auwera who was lying wounded in the hospital, Second Lieutenant Michaux, Lieutenant Polis, the recording secretary, Captain Hotermans, Lieutenant Verstraeten and First Sergeant Nystem.

Jottrand explained the situation as he knew it up to that moment. Then he read article 51 of the "Instruction on the defense of a fort.":

"The surrender of a fort is not justified unless it finds itself in one of the two following circumstances:

1. When all defensive means of the fort and of its personnel are useless and non-reparable.

2. When all means of subsistence of the garrison are exhausted."

Then he asked those assembled: "In view of the circumstances, what is your opinion about the possibility of continuing resistance?" Before Jottrand stood a group whose courage had been proved in the travail of the past 28 hours.

In unison, to Jottrand's astonishment, they unhesitatingly favored surrender! None were under pressure to take this stand, the regulations making it quite clear that each individual would make his own choice without undue influence by anyone. A statement that committed each one present to the agreement to surrender, was prepared, Jottrand asking each man to sign it. The next step was to establish terms of surrender. The Belgians debated the matter and decided on what could be reasonably demanded. They agreed that: The evacuation of the wounded be permitted; the garrison be allowed to live; and that the garrison be honorably treated in accordance with international agreements on prisoners of war. The council had met for 25 minutes. Jottrand now went into the tunnels, everyone there was intent on learning the provisions of the proposed surrender.

Jottrand followed the prescribed rules when he called the council but, inwardly, to the utter surprise and untold dismay of many, he had not lost his determination to be a good soldier to the end. In the tunnels he astounded the soldiers by saying "We are going to attempt to leave the Fort to rejoin the Belgian Army. I am your Commander and I will lead the way. Remember the fate of prisoners of war. Theirs is a sad, depressing lot, crushed, forced into privation, far from their homeland . . ." This was as far as he could get.

Cries of "We want to surrender! We want to live! We want to see our wives and loved ones again!" rose about him. This was Jottrand's most humiliating defeat. He could not compromise any longer. In one last desperate gesture, he got General Jadot's administrative officer on the telephone and again went through the situation. This was Jottrand's final conversation with a Higher Headquarters. Jadot would not permit surrender. He insisted the Fort must be destroyed first. The decision of the council was not to be backed up. Jottrand's dilemma had worsened. But he resolved to attempt to accomplish both a surrender and destruction to comply with the intent of Jadot's orders. Of the 17 major works of the Fort, seven still held out, their supplies dwindling, or gone, their crews badly battered, the guns less than effective, offering only light resistance to major German pressure.

Jottrand entrusted the surrender negotiations to Captain Hotermans. Hotermans was to bargain with the Germans long enough for Jottrand to destroy completely every work yet in operation.

As Jottrand later recalled: "It was not in the best interests of Belgium to send someone to surrender the Fort right then. It was better that someone would go to find the Commander of the attacking German troops and talk with him and return with officials properly appointed to start the final negotiations. A new meeting of the defense council would take place following the demands of the enemy—the council would accept or refuse. I estimated that this would take some time, time that I could use to good advantage." Whether Jottrand made this strategy known to his own negotiators, however, is a moot point.

Hotermans first went to the gunners in the casemate at the entrance. He ordered the crew to cease firing. Sergeant Debarsy, intently firing on a bridge across the Geer either did not, or did not choose to hear, Hotermans' repeated *"Cease fire:"* in a loud voice. He took the Sergeant by the arm and had to drag him from the gun seat. Reluctantly, Sergeant Borsu, manning the 60-mm cannon, and its crew chief, Sergeant Lecron, and two young Peeters brothers, left their weapons and withdrew into the interior of the Fort. The men under Sergeant Hermesse at another weapon did the same.

Debarsy remained with Hotermans. An escort of several soldiers who were to protect Hotermans as he left the Fort disappeared, and the party stood at four men: Hotermans, Sergeant Debarsy, Private Demoulin—the white flag in his hand—and the bugler, Vervier.

At this point events became confused. When Hotermans got to the gate, and it was lowered, he halted. He stood before the gate and refused to budge. Hotermans, in later testimony, stated that he felt the decision to surrender was premature and he would not be the agent of defeat. He was particularly upset that he should be burdened with the surrender since he was one of the first of three officers assigned to the Fort when it was commissioned. He had a sentimental attachment to Fort Eben Emael. He begged Jottrand to give the unenviable task to another. Jottrand then gave the mission to Lieutenant Vamecq who met Hotermans at the gate. Vamecq pleaded with Hotermans not to relinquish his mission.

Colonel Melzer had, by mid-morning, strengthened Mikosche's forces. A German artillery force, under Captain Hauboldt, located in and around the village of Eben Emael joined Mikosch. Hauboldt had sent some units skilled at destruction of armored emplacements, to rid the north wall of stubborn casemate seventeen. Other casemates also began to fall.

The Germans, on top of the Fort, could now hear explosions underground, not of their doing. Lieutenant Delcourt, on the orders of Major Jottrand, set out to destroy the electrical system except for whatever it would take to keep the minimum lighting in essential installations. Delcourt set off 20 pounds of

Discarded gear of Belgian prisoners. Casemate 3, the entrance to Eben Emael, is at top right. The remains of the barracks is at top left.

dynamite in all but one of the generators. Lieutenant Quitin worked frantically to destroy all machinery within the interior. He used crowbars, axes and sledge hammers on fuse boxes, power terminals, telephone switchboards and elevator mechanisms. By 1200 the incessant pounding of Hauboldt's guns caused the crew of cupola twenty-three to give up. The cupola's guns had served well. They had successfully blown the bridge at Lanaye. Sergeant Fourier set heavy charges against the guns, fused them, and then withdrew with his crew. One of them, Peletier, had served as an observer for 28 hours without relief. At a safe distance Peletier pulled a long cord strung through the tunnel, and attached to the fuses. The whole south end of the Fort trembled. This ended the life of the most stubborn and defiant of the Belgian works.

Thirty-three, the casemate that had stood up so well under Stuka attack the preceding day, finally found its guns inoperative from incessant attacks. Sergeant Janviers and his crew withdrew into the Fort's interior. Although the Belgians had orders to blow casemate nine, and made strenuous efforts to carry out the order, something went wrong and the charges in the guns never went off. The Germans found this position intact.

When notified by messenger to destroy his guns Sergeant Flamand refused, saying he had to have a personal order from an officer. That was that! No officer dared to argue with him.

Jottrand ordered Lieutenant Gigot to blow up the 120's. Gigot reported back later that to do an effective job of destruction it would take at least an hour and a half. He would have to surmount the barriers, move the heavy charges, go through tortuous and unlighted passageways, up stairways with many treads missing, to reach the firing chambers and set explosives in the guns.

At 1210 the 120-mm gun cupola had not yet been destroyed. Jottrand sent Dehousse and six of the non-commissioned officers to assist Gigot in moving the explosives forward and up to the gun turret and prepare for its destruction. At about that time, Private Ancia, who, throughout the defense had conducted himself in an exemplary manner, came to Jottrand saying, "I will take care of the destruction of casemate thirty-three. I will do whatever is necessary, leave it to me!" What was lacking, apparently, was a battery to set off the charge that had already been set in place.

Ancia dashed to the power central and into the maintenance shop where he located a battery, and dashed back, past bewildered and downcast comrades. Several minutes later—everyone heard the explosion come from thirty-three. A sergeant returning from the tunnel falsely claimed that he had blown the position. Ancia never returned. The Sergeant later recanted his story. It was Ancia who had blown up the casemate and blown himself into oblivion!

This incident, because of the magnitude of the tragedy that was occurring elsewhere, was not immediately reported. It was only days later, on the long trek to Fallingbostel, that the truth about Ancia's heroism became known to the Belgian prisoners. Ancia's sacrifice was the last gesture of defiance from the Belgian garrison.

15. SURRENDER

At about 1215, the Germans began to hear a frail, flute-like ound that penetrated the cracking bullets and the burst of rtillery and antitank guns. Undaunted, it eerily resounded cross the countryside, becoming louder and clearer as German fter German lowered his sights and listened to its haunting vail. Vervier, standing ramrod straight in the recesses of the ate, in terrible danger that he would be killed by ricocheting ullets or blinded by flying concrete chips, blew his bugle as he ad never had before. He sounded a military call he had never xpected to play. He was sounding surrender! Within the Fort he tunnel reverberated the sound. He blew many minutes. The ullets ceased hitting near the entrance and the earth stopped rembling as the artillery fire dwindled. Then there was silence xcept for his call for men to stop this particular war. When e ceased blowing a deathly stillness settled over the countryside.

Captain Vamecq came from behind Vervier. Demoulin, arrying the white flag, passed over the drawbridge and set the lag against the wall just outside the entrance. The Germans saw he Captain in the entranceway and signaled him to advance. Vamecq went forward. The bridge was raised behind him. He valked ahead to a gate and faced the Germans with Vervier, he bugler, at his side.

The Captain, in accordance with instructions from the Germans, surrendered his pistol. A French-speaking German

officer appeared. The Captain pulled out the bolt of the gat
and opened it. He stepped forward and the gate closed auto
matically behind him, but no one locked it.

The Belgian Captain told the Germans that the Fort wa
surrendering and requested military honors and the evacuatio
of the wounded. Two Germans led Vamecq towards the bridg
over the Geer, to meet the German Commander to discus
surrender. But before he had gone very far, he looked back
He could not believe what was occurring, nor how it coul
happen. Hundreds of Belgians, arms raised above their heads
were filing from the Fort!

A German non-commissioned officer had opened the gate
and ordered a Belgian to lower the drawbridge. The Belgia
complied, and without much further ado, Belgians standing a
the foot of the bridge in the interior of the Fort, began to fil
out into the open air, thinking a surrender had been agree
upon. German soldiers, guns at the ready, made their wa
through the disorderly ranks of Belgians filing out, and pene
trated the interior of the Fort.

At 1217 below the Command Post, Lieutenant Dehouss
got word of what was happening at the exit. He made his wa
to the level above to the Command Post to inform Majo
Jottrand. To confirm the report, Jottrand picked up the telephon
and tried to reach the guard room at the gate, but withou
success. He then tried to reach Liège to give them the situation
but Lieutenant Delrez, who was trying to get Liège on the tele
phone for the Major, found that although the line seeme
open, no one responded. Nevertheless, on the instructions o
Jottrand he said, "We have surrendered!" It was 1227. Lièg
did not respond. Both officers then went to work as rapidly a
possible to knock out the telephones and burn secret materials.

Gigot, coming from the 120-mm cupola for more explosives
unaware of events at the entrance of the Fort, ran into men
hands raised above their heads. He reeled backward in utte

shock as it suddenly dawned on him what was taking place. Men shouted, "We have surrendered!" Gigot turned a deaf ear intent on carrying out his mission. He returned to the cupola where he found Polis. They both concluded that it would be impossible to carry out Jottrand's order. They therefore returned to Hotermans' office where they found Lieutenant De Sloovere, Verstraeten and Legaie. Disconsolately, they all trudged towards the exit of the Fort. The 120-mm guns, as mentioned earlier, had been sorely damaged by Witzig's men the previous day. It was very doubtful that the weapons could ever have been reconditioned. The blowing of the cupola, if indeed it could have been done, would have been nothing more than a thumbing the nose at the Germans, a vacant self-abnegating gesture by the Belgians, better left undone.

Jottrand and Delrez, the destruction of papers completed, wended their way through the dark debris-strewn tunnels below and passed the workshop where a German soldier stood. Jottrand managed to make him understand that he would like to go to his quarters and get his personal things. He was allowed to do so. As he moved about his quarters, he made a last check to see that everything of value to the enemy had been destroyed. He heard some voices in the tunnel outside his billet, and found the doctors and their aid men removing the wounded. Jottrand followed the last of the wounded, past Germans standing guard. The Germans were in a jovial mood but all conducted themselves decorously towards the badly mauled and downcast Belgians. Outside, he found many of his officers, weaponless and despondent. Ranks were forming for the march to the village.

A German officer approached Major Jottrand. It was Colonel Mikosch. "Major Jottrand," he said, "will you give me your word of honor that you have placed no delayed mines within the Fort?"

"There are none. I give you my word of honor." Jottrand answered in a broken voice. Jottrand could give this word unequivocally because the Belgians had no such weapons within the Fort.

Colonel Mikosch walked over to the Belgian officers. He said, "I congratulate you on your courage. Someone must be defeated in war. I am sorry this must happen to you. But this is war. I must send you to Germany."

Witzig had his force collect their gear and assemble. Witzig had lost 26 men, about a third of his force in something over a day of combat. Six were dead. Granite had paid a big price for victory. At 1400, after the dead were buried, Witzig's Force made its way to the area near the entrance of the Fort, with 30 Belgian prisoners. Witzig turned them over to a Captain Hauboldt, one of Mikosch's officers.

Some of Witzig's men joined the group under Hauboldt's command. A gliderman impishly asked one of Hauboldt's men, "Do you know the name of this Fort?"

"No," came the response.

"You don't?" his eyebrows raised. "Why, it's Fort Eben Emael."

Witzig marched his men past the Loverix Mill, that was now a shell, badly torn by guns from the Fort as well as artillery and Stuka bombs, and on into the village of Eben Emael. There the men found what they then sought most—a "bierstube" and drank beer to their heart's content to slake a day's thirst. They relaxed there several hours, long enough to know that the work they had started at 0430, the day before, was now being completed by German ground troops. This they knew for they were roused from the tavern by the sound of marching men. The defeated, downcast defenders of that great Fortress, a column almost a mile long, marched by. As the Germans watched the end of the column come into view, they saw a blond head bobbing unevenly above the heads of the prisoners. As it drew close they saw a child, a very young child, riding the shoulders of a broad-shouldered Belgian non-commissioned officer. Her hands were tightly clasped around his head. Alefs waved at her. She smiled but would not let go to wave back.

On the way through Maastricht, the Germans insisted that Sergeant Lecron must leave his daughter. A German officer arranged for her to be taken to a convent, and Sergeant Lecron finally let her go. She was later located there by her grandfather who, for two years, had bicycled from convent to convent, in search of his little grandaughter. He took her to his home. She is now married and has three children of her own to grace Sergeant Lecron's old age.

In the late afternoon the glidermen drove in to Aachen en route to their barracks in Ostheim. German civilians, seeing these odd, disheveled characters shook their fists in hate, under the impression that they were enemy prisoners. Suddenly, they saw that the glidermen were carrying guns and bandoliers of ammunition. "They are not the enemy! They are Germans!" Hisses turned to cheers.

As these events were taking place, Mikosch's men went about the job of securing their prize. They searched the Fort completely, every tunnel, every gun chamber, and made an inventory of all equipment. Later, many of the guns that remained serviceable or reparable found their way into German units on the Russian front.

Late in the search, some of the Germans heard muffled cries and pounding of metal against metal in one of the casemates. They went in the direction of the sound—it came from a small room, the casemate's telephone switchboard room. Prying open the door they found two terrified, young and very hungry Belgians. They were Noel and Petit.

Led by Lieutenant Witzig, the men of the glider assault force marc[h] toward Maastricht after being relieved by German ground forces o[n] May 11th. Gliderman with bandaged head is Sergeant Wenzel.

16. HITLER'S MILITARY GENIUS

Seventy-seven boldly led men, 10 gliders costing about 77,000 Deutschmarks, and 56 hollow charge explosives defeated 780 men defending the world's strongest fort. The Fort fell in somewhat more than a day, but the decisive struggle took place during the first 20 minutes. Contrasting the small amount of resources used by the Germans and the brilliance of the victory, there is no similar accomplishment to equal it in history. It was the prelude to British debacle at Dunkerque and the downfall of France. General Karl von Clausewitz had many years ago stated that there is a key to every country. Fort Eben Emael was the key to Belgium and, in a larger sense, it unlocked the door to the West. The capture of the Fort was, in itself, an important military feat. In a broad sense, and in view of what was taking place elsewhere on the 10th and 11th of May, the importance of the victory may not have been evident at the time and now may be ignored by many.

The taking of the bridges at Veldwezelt and Vroenhoven were important in a tactical sense and, in some respects, overshadowed the taking of the Fort. In the strategic and political sense, the fall of Fort Eben Emael had substantially greater importance and meaning. Had the Fort not fallen to Witzig, its guns would have played havoc with the German ground Blitzkrieg in the area around Eben Emael. It might have cost the

Germans heavily in men and time to reduce it by a groun
attack. Once the resistance of the Fort had been destroyed, th
Germans surged through the gaps between Maastricht and Ebe
Emael, on to Liège and into the interior of Belgium. This mov
destroyed any effort on the part of the Belgian Army to make
meaningful riposte, and stave off military and political disaster
The road to the Channel was clear and the British escape throug
Dunkerque an unavoidable consequence.

Important though a victory at Fort Eben Emael was i
fostering military aims, its supreme value lay in its political re
sults. For several hours after 0530, the 10th of May, Belgium'
King and Parliament were not abreast of Witzig's progress. Th
Belgian High Command refused to be realistic, their reports t
King and Parliament conveying a false optimism. When the trut
started to become known, that the Fort was not merely in seriou
trouble, but had capitulated, Belgian morale began to crack, fo
to the Belgians, Fort Eben Emael was virtually holy ground
An enemy had dared to take it and had succeeded. Added t
this shock, rumors beset the nation. The bastion had fallen wit
breathtaking speed, by the use of mysterious weapons. A delug
of demoralizing rumors swept the nation and France, across th
Channel and soon the Atlantic. The image of Nazi militar
prowess, if not invincible, was not soon to be dispelled. The she
of Fort Eben Emael became a showpiece of Nazi military might
and it served to weld stronger the Axis bonds.

Fort Eben Emael was the prelude not only to Dunkerqu
but also to four bitter years of war that might have been avoide
had the Fort held for as little as several days. Had it done s
the character of the war might have altered. It would hav
slowed General von Kluck's blitzkrieg through Belgium. Only
few days would have allowed the Belgians, French and Britis
time to take counter measures.

Some Belgian officers contend that Fort Eben Emael wa

a good Fort in a defective defensive system. Some say it was a bad Fort. Perhaps there is an element of truth in both statements. The first group would contend that such a Fort should never have been built on the frontier. Smaller defenses would have been better. The Fort was actually not on the Belgian-German frontier. It was 15 miles to the Dutch-German frontier. Theoretically, Dutch resistance should have served to protect the Fort. The Fort never had a fair chance to prove its muscle. Not even a fighting chance against the new approach to war.

Fort Eben Emael was primarily an artillery position, and its first mission was to place artillery fire on the enemy attacking other Belgian units and forts such as Barchon and Pontisse, or trying to seize the important bridges over the Meuse. Secondarily, it formed a part of the network of forts, pillboxes, and casemates set at tactically critical points along the frontier. It was not expected to come under infantry attack immediately. This also helps to explain the failure of the Belgian artillery in the Fort to mount effective infantry-style counter attacks. These attacks were conducted not by infantrymen but artillerymen, heroically led but, on the whole, poorly organized and executed, using faulty tactics.

Even if Dutch resistance had been weak, nevertheless, the Germans would have had to regroup to make the necessary preparations to cross the Albert Canal. Some indication of the validity of this viewpoint is borne out in the amount of time it took relief forces to get to the Fort. Had the German invasion been primarily a ground blitzkrieg, Belgian pride in Fort Eben Emael as a bastion of defense would have been vindicated, for Fort Eben Emael's guns would have wreaked havoc on German columns, and have delayed, perhaps by days, the advances of the Germans through that zone.

No fort is perfect. Fort Eben Emael was not a perfect fort, but it was a good fort. It was manned by brave men. It had excellent weapons. It was, tactically, well organized and designed. The Belgians should have heavily mined and booby trapped the areas around the casemates and cupolas. There could have been more barbed wire, antiaircraft machine guns, and better coordination with infantry regiments to help counterattack the paratroopers.

It was a superb Fort in every sense by World War I standards, a good Fort for Word War II. The problem was not one of valor, material or casemates, or defective design. The problem lay in men's minds and, quite specifically, in Belgian staff and top command minds. As Philip Wylie states, "The military mind is . . . a habit—a custom—a tradition—a mental stasis." The Belgians failed to find out about gliders, or try to imagine such a weapon. Had they done so, they could have foreseen and contested a glider landing. They had thought about an enemy parachute attempt but rightfully discounted it as impractical or suicidal to the enemy. The hollow charge is another matter entirely. Only a highly-advanced military, scientifically strong nation might have invented this lethal device before or at the same time as the Germans and guessed its use on such a surface as the Fort.

Fort Eben Emael was built prior to a historical turning point in warfare and its creators were idea poor. They were not visionaries. Visionary, creative leaders win wars or prevent defeat. It was an idea that was far ahead of its time that made the capture of Fort Eben Emael possible. The idea was that an airborne attack using gliders should be made. The landing implemented the idea and the battle results confirmed its wisdom. At 0450, 10 May 1940, about 20 minutes after the last glider had discharged its squad, warfare had forever changed in character.

Time, circumstances and Hitler's intellect fated Belgium to be the victim. More defenders, more guns, earlier alerting of the men, more coordinated counterattacks, nothing, absolutely nothing, could have altered what occurred. Belgium was a victim on whom a new type of warfare was successfully tried.

Without the 110-pound hollow charge to knock out the steel cupolas and observation turrets there is serious question whether the guns of Eben Emael could have been silenced, or if most of the casemates could have been neutralized so rapidly. More glider loads of conventional explosives alone would not have been the answer. 4,000 conventionally armed Germans on the surface could never have intimidated the Belgian garrison. The Germans could not have succeeded in this venture without the hollow charge nor could they have succeeded without the glider. There was no way to lower the hollow charges onto the surface of the Fort except by glider. Gliders answered a need parachutes could not. The ground shock of a parachute drop could damage hollow charges, and there was no certainty they could be dropped within the Fort's perimeter.

By 1940 parachuting techniques had been well developed in both Germany and Russia. Men and equipment could be dropped, but nothing then nor since had been devised to eliminate the wide scattering of men and equipment during a drop and the time consuming assembly subsequently required.

Certainly, a parachute drop on Fort Eben Emael, for reasons given here, was not the answer to German requirements. Although the Belgians could have guessed the Germans, in a desperate gamble to capture the Fort, might try an air drop technique, the glider was the unexpected surprise.

In historical retrospect, all phases of the operation from its intellectual conception to the final invasion of the Fort by Mikosch's forces proved sound. In some details, however, the Germans committed notable errors, particularly in their intelligence estimates. These misled Lieutenant Witzig and caused him, in several instances, to allocate his slender resources improperly.

Intelligence concerning the enemy in any combat situation is, by and large, hardly ever perfect, and never sufficient for a commander. General von Clausewitz's dictum put it well when he said, "War is the province of uncertainty; three-fourths of the things on which action is based lie hidden in the fog of a greater or less uncertainty." Thus it was with this operation to some extent. On the planning side of the venture, gliders had never been used in combat and timing of their landing was a hazardous guess, for on timing depended much of the surprise, not only of the attack at Fort Eben Emael, but along the whole front.

Victory in war is the ultimate gauge of military wisdom. Measured by this time-honored standard, Hitler's scoffed-at decision to attack Fort Eben Emael by vertical envelopment, despite the odds against its success, was eminently sound.

General Student's belief that "the capture of Fort Eben Emael is the greatest military victory that man has ever won," will gradually take hold as information concerning its many achievements become known and understood. Also, whatever the implications, men can no longer discount the genius of Hitler, genius of savagery though it was.

I trust that some day Belgian's self doubt and embarrassment will dissolve. In its place will come, I hope, pride and respect for every man who fought that day. Even though Jottrand was not disgraced, and as a matter of fact was promoted to lieutenant colonel, he did carry a heavy burden to his grave. I trust his nation will some day accord him the honor and distinction due a soldier who did his duty as best he knew. Certainly no one could have done more, for no one else stood so alone at the threshold of a dramatic change in the art of war.

17. EPILOGUE

Several days after the platoon returned to the "Flak Caserne," Witzig received orders from recently-promoted Major Koch to report with other officers of Task Force Koch for special ceremonies. There Adolf Hitler addressed them and then presented each officer with the Ritterkreuz (Knight's Cross), Nazi Germany's highest combat decoration. In separate ceremonies, General Kesserling decorated each enlisted man with the Iron Cross. In addition to this award, each soldier was promoted one grade—all except Grechza, the soldier with the rum-spiked canteen who dared to straddle the Fort's greatest gun.

Soon orders transferring the men to other units where their skills and experience were needed began to dismember Witzig's force. In a few months the last of its men had departed and the unit was deactivated.

Early in 1941 Hitler ordered an attack on the Greek Island of Crete. It was to be history's first full-scale airborne invasion. Men like those of Task Force Granite were urgently needed. The General Staff placed a high priority on locating them and issuing the necessary orders to bring them into the airborne units being formed for the invasion. Soon many of them were together again. On 21 May 1941 they landed on Crete, this time most of them were dropped by parachute. Most of the glider pilots also participated. Heiner Lange was at the controls of the

Adolf Hitler with officers of Assault Force Granite at his headquarters. The first three officers from the left are Delica, Witzig, and Koch.

glider carrying Major Koch. "Captain" Witzig went into action by parachute as did Sergeant Wenzel. Although 15,000 German airborne troops defeated a force almost three times their number, the Germans lost 5,000 killed and wounded and a large number of aircraft. Largely because of the frightful losses Hitler became disenchanted with airborne operations. He also felt that after Fort Eben Emael and Crete, such operations had lost the element of surprise in warfare. Thus, he never again gave serious attention to this aspect of warfare.

Sergeant Wenzel, after two years of combat experience, rose to the rank of Captain. The Americans captured him in North Africa. He was shipped to the United States and spent the last three years of the war as a prisoner in Camp Crossville, Tennessee. After Crete, Witzig fought in Russia and later served in a staff position in France. He is now a Colonel in the German Army and a director at the Engineer School near Munich, Germany.

Until his untimely death in 1942, Major Koch met from time to time with Witzig and other comrades to reminisce on their historic venture and perhaps discuss some newly hatched scheme. The possible capture of Gibraltar was a favorite topic.

For many hours Koch and Heiner Lange studied the topography of the "Rock", its prevailing winds, the dimensions of its few level surfaces where gliders could land and, more important, "if" they could land on the rocky promontory. Heiner Lange figured he would be able to bring a glider down safely on some of the steep slopes by landing at an uphill angle. However, when Franco politely but firmly told Adolf Hitler that if an attack were to be launched the Spanish would do it, they reluctantly dropped further discussion as pointless but not before Koch had pretty well concluded that such an operation could be carried out successfully.

Soon restive minds turned to their greatest adventure, a

landing in the heart of London to spirit away Winston Churchill from the chambers of the House of Parliament. When questioned about the operation in 1970 General Student brushed it off as pure fantasy by over-enthusiastic youngsters. Nevertheless, Major Koch, Heiner Lange and a small coterie dreamed of having a go at it. They conjured up many ideas including a plan they felt would make it workable. Heiner Lange recalled some of its details.

Aerial photographs disclosed a long, triangular piece of greenery adjoining the Houses of Parliament. It appeared to be suitable for glider landings. They would arrive when Parliament was in session. The glidermen, faces blackened and wearing smoked glasses would break into Parliament and then fire brilliant flares to temporarily blind Churchill and others in the chamber. With all entrances covered, a picked group would grab Churchill and take him to one of the several Storch airplanes that would accompany the attackers and fly the Prime Minister to Germany.

In 1964 Heiner Lange, who speaks English fluently, was in London as an interpreter for a German official. He had long forgotten the wild plan. They were in a cab traveling to an appointment at one of the British ministries when Heiner Lange saw the triangle of green come into view against a backdrop of the weathered facade of the Houses of Parliament. Suddenly, the planned adventure in all its detail, rose in Lange's mind. To his horror, as they drove closer to the park, instead of a nice grassy uncluttered area, he saw high trees and sturdy monuments. The landing would have been a disaster. Or would it have been?

"Had the trees perhaps grown since?" I asked Lange.

He lifted his eyebrows, "Well, possibly. There might have been a slight chance".

It would have been risky, yes, but no more so than the daring glider operation in 1944 that spirited Mussolini from a hotel on a 10,000-foot peak in the Grand Sasso where he was a prisoner. It was classed by Mussolini as "Modern in method and style, and the boldest, most romantic escape and rescue in this epoch of history." But that is another story.

Pleased with the DFS 230, and eager to exploit the tactical potential the glider offered in airborne assaults, the German High Command pushed for more gliders to support future airborne operations. Transport glider developments moved apace. The quality of ingenuity and enterprise displayed by the Germans in their DFS 230 program continued with many other models. One, the Gigant, was enormous, carrying as many as 200 soldiers. It was towed by three two-motored He 111's and later by a specially built He 111 that had two fuselages and five motors. Another small "Kamhose" glider was designed to dive at 500 miles per hour and plunge, kamikaze-style, into enemy bomber formations.

Hundreds of gliders were marshalled on the airfields of France to carry the vanguard of the German forces on their way to England. Soon after Hitler called off the invasion of England German gliders were on their way over the Aegean to land men and guns on Crete. After Crete, gliders were no longer used on a large scale. However, they continued to haul men and guns to the far reaches of Hitler's expanding empire. GO 242's, some DFS 230's and a few ME 321 gliders flew to Rommel's assistance. Towed by the Ju 52, Heiner Lange flew twenty supply missions at the controls of the GO 242 carrying a variety of guns and equipment to Rommel. To avoid radar detection tug and glider skimmed 1000 miles five feet over the Mediterranean. During five grueling hours Lange had to keep both hands on the controls to maintain this dangerous altitude. Any lapse in attention, any letting go of the controls could prove disastrous as, he learned when he took a swat at a nagging fly, to find the fuselage sliding along the water throwing spray like the prow of a speed boat, in the split second it took him to swat and grab the controls again.

These gliders flew many thousands of miles into the heart of Russia on virtual suicide missions supplying critically needed food and munitions to isolated pockets of Germans. The pilots remained in most cases to fight alongside their comrades, their fate either death or surrender and a harrowing march into the Siberian wilderness to prison.

Hanna Reitsch, as a test pilot on the Staff of General Udet, continued testing new German gliders. As the tide of battle began to turn in favor of the Allies, and Hitler sought to bring new weapons into being that would stem the Allied tide, the aviatrix took over the dangerous job of flying experimental models of the notorious V-1 glide bomb that was soon to terrorize London and hit strategic targets in England. At the controls of a V I armed with a dummy warhead, the daring aviatrix was towed into the air where she performed a range of tests while under tow and in free glide and diving flights. She was with Hitler and his staff in the bunker at the Reichs Chancellery until two days before Hitler committed suicide.

In creating the hollow charge, the Germans had taken an important stride towards discovering the principal of atomic fission. Fortunately, however, Hitler's scientists met with technical problems they were unable to solve in time to prevent the United States from dropping the atom bomb on Japan.

ADDENDUM

In 1945, the U. S. freed Helmut Wenzel from the prisoner of war camp in Tennessee and he returned to Germany to become a career Foerster, managing wild game and timber farms. He likes to be called Jaeger, a professional hunter, but officially has attained the position of Aberfoerster, superintendant in his profession. He lives with his wife, two sons and a daughter in a rustic ranch house on the outskirts of Celle. Colonel Rudolf Witzig is on active duty in the German Army and is a director of a key staff of the Engineer School near Munich. General Kurt Student lives in retirement in Bad Salzuflen, is 80, and in excellent health. Rudolf Opitz is an engineer with Avco Corporation in Stratford, Connecticut and heads that company's helicopter engine test and development programs. Dr. Alexander Lippisch for a period after the war worked as a consultant for the U. S. aircraft and electronic industries and his talent was used in limited areas of the space program.

Jean De Sloovere, retired a major, is a civil engineer for an industrial association and lives in Brussels, Belgium. Alfred Hotermans, also retired, lives close by and works as an office manager for a firm of American attorneys.

Heiner Lange told me that Hitler first became aware of the

glider in 1936 at the annual Reichsparteitag festival in Nuremburg, Germany. As part of the program, planes released three gliders piloted by Brautigan, Hesse and another pilot high above the stadium. The gliders drew awed attention and spontaneous, wild applause from the onlookers jamming the stands as the gliders stunted gracefully. The final maneuver was to be a formation fly by skimming the top of the stands to land on a field beyond. Anxious to give Hitler a convincing demonstration of the glider's capabilities, the three made a dramatic sweep into the bowl to bring their craft to a halt in front of the box of a surprised Hitler and his retinue. Their feat proved the highlight of the festivities.

One bleak day in December 1969 I visited the isolated, decaying Fort Eben Emael in a staff car generously provided by the Belgian Army. I was intent on this visit in locating the house of Sergeant Lecron. I crossed the Geer at the Loverix Mill. A peasant, the only human I could see, was working a small plot about 150 yards from the entrance to the Fort. I got out of the car called, "Où est la maison Lecron?"

"Ici," he answered and pointed to a small bare field just adjacent.

"Mais où est la maison?" I asked for I saw no house.

Again he said, "Ici."

The house was gone. I learned later that its gaunt walls were torn down shortly after the war.

GLOSSARY

Bangalore Torpedo	A metal tube or pipe that is packed with a high explosive charge usually used to blow pathways through barbed wire.
Caponiere	A watch tower jutting from the wall of a fort with slit-like openings, (embrasures) from which observers can watch for an approaching enemy or from which weapons can be fired. Also similar to a blockhouse.
Casemate	A bombproof structure protecting guns, troops or ammunition.
Casern(e)	A barracks or building for housing soldiers.
Cupola	An armored turret that may house artillery or be used as an observation dome.
DFS	Deutsche Forschungsanstalt Fuer Segelflug—German Research Institute for gliders.

DFS 230	A German transport glider able to carry 10 men or an equivalent weight.
Embrasure	An opening in a wall or parapet through which a gun is fired.
GO 242	A German glider built by the Gotha (GO) factory, able to transport 30 soldiers or an equivalent weight or cargo.
HE 111	A German bomber built by the Henkel factory.
Ju 52	A German transport airplane built in the Junker factory used extensively as a glider tow plane.
Machine pistol	A name applied to one of many makes of automatic pistol to which a shoulder piece can be attached so that the weapon can be used as a shoulder-fired weapon. Such a weapon uses a magazine containing as many as 30 cartridges and has a rate of fire reaching 600 rounds per minute.
ME 321	A German glider built by the Messerschmidt Company able to transport 200 men or an equivalent weight up to 20 tons of materiel.
Paraengineer	An engineer trained soldier equipped to land behind enemy

lines from airplanes by means of parachutes.

Paratrooper	A soldier trained and equipped to land behind enemy lines from airplanes by means of parachutes. All paratroopers landing on Fort Eben Emael were trained paraengineers.
Section	A tactical military unit smaller than a platoon and larger than a squad.
Squad	A small tactical unit, on a command level below the platoon, consisting of only as many men, usually no more than eight, that a leader can direct easily in the field.
Stuka	A German dive bomber of World War II.
Sturmabteilung	Storm Group. "Abteilung" usually refers to a unit the size of a battalion.
Sturmgruppe	An assault group somewhat larger than a platoon.

BIBLIOGRAPHY

BOOKS

Bekker, Cajus. *Luftwaffe War Diaries.* Translated and edited by Frank Zeigler, London: McDonald, 1967.

Clausewitz, Karl von. *On War.* Translated from the German by O. J. Matthijs Jolles: Washington, D. C. Infantry Journal Press, 1950.

Foley, Charles. *Commando Extraordinary,* London: Longmans, Green and Company, 1954.

Groueff, Stephane. *Manhattan Project, The Untold Story of the Making of the Atomic Bomb.* New York: Little, Brown & Co., 1967.

Groves, Leslie. *Now It Can Be Told, The Story of the Manhattan Project.* New York: Harper and Brothers, 1962.

Lhoest, Jean-Louis. *Les Paras Allemands au Canal Albert.* Paris: Presses de la Cité, 1964.

Horne, Alistair. *To Lose a Battle.* Boston: Little Brown and Company, 1969.

Meesen, L. *Ce Que J'ai Vu A Eben-Emael.* Liège: Collection Nationale Civisme, 1953.

Melzer, Walter. *Albert Kanal und Eben-Emael.* Frankfurt: Kurt Wohlwinckel, 1957.

Morzik, Fritz. *Die Deutschen Transportflieger im Zweiten Welt-krieg.* Frankfurt: Bernard & Graefe, 1966.

Mrazek, James E. *The Art of Winning Wars.* New York: Walker and Company, 1969.

———. *World War II Glider Operations,* in preparation.

Reitsch, Hanna. *Flying is My Life.* Translated by Lawrence Wilson, New York: G. P. Putnam, 1954.

Rickenbacker, Edward V. *Seven Came Through.* New York: Doubleday and Doran, 1943.

Shirer, William L. *The Rise and Fall of the Third Reich.* New York: Simon and Schuster, 1960.

Wylie, Philip. "Military Men," from *Man and Warfare.* Edited by William F. Irmscher, Boston: Little Brown and Company, 1964.

ARTICLES

Buchner, R. Alex. "Der Feldwebel Portsteffen," *Soldat und Technik,* April, 1969, pp. 208-209.

Dach, Hans von. "Luftlandeangriff auf einen befestigten Flussab-schnitt," *Der Schweizer Soldat Wehrzeitung,* Zurich, 28 February 1969, pp. 35-70.

Kurz, H. R. "Die Operation Eben Emael," *Allgemeine Schweizer Militarzeit Schrift.*

Pissen, Werner. "Die Einnahme der Festung Eben-Emael am 10/11

Mai 1940," *Allgemeine Schweizerische Militaer Zeitschrift,* Août, 1959, pp. 579-589.

Schacht, Gerhard, "Eben-Emael, 10 Mai, 1940," *Wehrwissenschaftliche Rundschau,* Mai, 1954, pp. 217-223.

Witzig Rudolf. "Eben Emael," *Pioniere,* February 1965, pp. 50-59.

REPORTS

Combat reports in German of Sergeants Niedermeier, Arendt, and Wenzel, dated September 1941 prepared in compliance with a directive of a board of investigation established to examine the combat performance of certain members of Storm Group Granite.

Evaluation Reports in German made by each squad leader of Storm Group Granite prepared during May 1940 at Hildesheim, Germany after Fort Eben Emael had been captured.

Extract from the war diary of Lieutenant Rudolf Witzig in German between dates 6 May 1940 to 13 May 1940.

History of Fort Eben Emael prepared by Captain A. Hotermans while a prisoner of the Germans at Fallingbostel, Germany.

Journal de Campagne, Fort d'Eben-Emael Reconstitué en Captivité au Camp de Fallingbostel Suivant les Temoignes des Chefs d'Ouvrages et Officiers de Fort, enclosure to Bulletin Trimestriel No. 3, Août 1966, Ceux du Fort d'Eben-Emael, edited by G. Wilkin, Liège.

Report written by Rudolf Opitz, "Operation Fort Eben Emael, Belgium, 10 May 1940," Headquarters Air Material Command, Wright Field, Dayton, Ohio, September 1947. Re: TSDIN-2/JSH/dm.

STUDIES

Suchenwirth, Richard. "The Development of the German Air Force, 1919-1939," edited by Harry R. Fletcher, USAF Historical Division, USAF Historical Studies: No. 160, p. 236.

INTERVIEWS

General Oberst Kurt Student (ret.) Bad Salzuflen, Germany, 9 January 1970.
Heiner Lange, Augsburg, Germany, 2 January 1970.
Colonel Rudolf Witzig, Munich, Germany, 2 June 1969, 5 January 1970.
Rudolf Opitz, Stratford, Conn., 2 June 1970.
Helmut Wenzel, Celle, Germany 29-30 December 1970.
Jean De Sloovere, Brussels, 26 December 1969.
Alfred Hotermans, Brussels, 27 December 1970.
Edgard Levaque, Liège, Belgium, 21 December 1970.
Henri Decluse, Liège, Belgium (seven occasions 1969-1970).